INDIVIDUAL TO COLLECTIVE

Published by:
ORO Editions
Publishers of Architecture, Art, and Design
Gordon Goff: Publisher
www.oroeditions.com
info@oroeditions.com

Copyright © 2014 by ORO Editions
ISBN: 978-1-941806-08-1
10 09 08 07 06 5 4 3 2 1 First Edition

Book Design:
Pablo Mandel / CircularStudio.com

The texts are set in *Avenir,* a geometric sans-serif typeface
designed by Adrian Frutiger.

Color Separations and Printing:
ORO Group Ltd. Printed in China.

This book was printed and bound using a variety of sustainable manufacturing processes and materials including, aqueous-based
varnish, VOC- and formaldehyde-free glues, and phthalate-free laminations. The text is printed using offset sheet-fed lithographic
printing process in four color on 157gsm premium matte art paper with an off-line gloss aqueous spot varnish applied to all
photographs.

ORO Group Ltd. makes a continuous effort to minimize the overall carbon footprint of its publications. As part of this goal, ORO Group
Ltd. in association with Global ReLeaf, arranges to plant trees to replace those used in the manufacturing of the paper produced
for its books. Global ReLeaf is an international campaign run by American Forests, one of the world's oldest nonprofit conservation
organizations. Global ReLeaf is American Forests' education and action program that helps individuals, organizations, agencies, and
corporations improve the local and global environment by planting and caring for trees. Visit https://www.americanforests.org/our-
programs/global-releaf-projects/ for more details.

Library of Congress data: Available upon request.

For information on our distribution, please visit our website
www.oroeditions.com

INDIVIDUAL TO COLLECTIVE

DUDA/PAINE ARCHITECTS

FOREWORD by CESAR PELLI
EDITED by REBECCA W. E. EDMUNDS

CONTENTS

1

2

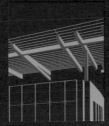

FOREWORD

The practice of architecture has changed much in the last 30 years and it is still changing. It has been affected by computer technology, above all. It has also been affected by globalization, by changes in the way buildings are financed and built, and by changes within the practice itself.

The way the profession is organized to produce its work has changed much, most notably by the emergence of huge professional firms with hundreds and sometimes thousands of employees, multiple disciplines, multiple offices, multiple owners, and multiple designers. These large firms have expanded and proliferated because they have several competitive advantages (also several disadvantages), but at the same time we have seen that smaller firms such as Duda/Paine Architects thrive by providing high-quality design and services. These smaller firms have attracted important clients who seek a more intimate and creative process. They offer a well-designed building, sometimes a very beautiful one, and very good attentive service. Duda/Paine Architects is one of those special firms.

I have known Turan Duda since he was a student at the Yale University School of Architecture while I was its dean. He later worked with me at Cesar Pelli & Associates for some 17 years. He was one of our top designers, a very bright, creative and engaging architect. Jeffrey Paine also worked at Cesar Pelli & Associates for over 15 years as a project manager. He was talented, well organized and courteous; excellent in his role. I knew from the moment they opened their firm, Duda/Paine Architects, that they made a very strong team of complimentary talents and inclinations which would meld into a distinctive practice. I knew also that because of their personalities they would offer very good service to their clients.

Turan Duda and Jeff Paine are talented, thoughtful, responsible architects and very good listeners. They are also both charming and gracious. These are not casual attributes for an architectural firm, but rather essential to the practice. For the institutions, organizations and individuals that become their clients, this means a design process that is comfortable and creative, buildings and spaces that are functional, elegant and well-built. This is, indeed, what Duda/Paine has been doing very successfully for 15 years.

The work here represents well what the firm has done. No doubt much more is in store. I know that as new work comes along their range of solutions and forms will keep on expanding.

I admire Duda/Paine not just because of the beautiful buildings they design, but because of the quality of the firm itself as a place where young architects can learn and grow. Turan Duda, particularly, is an excellent teacher and mentor. I believe that a nurturing place is a creative place, just what Duda/Paine Architects is.

— Cesar Pelli FAIA RIBA JIA

INTERVIEW

In the realm of architecture, the work of Duda/Paine Architects is remarkable in its diversity of location, scale and building type. However, it is even more remarkable when one understands that it emerged from Turan Duda and Jeff Paine's equal and unequivocal dedication to ideas and to the experience of individuals and communities. Within this volume are projects that span the globe, but are singularly contextual, that unite with the ground and soar into the sky, that provide quiet refuge, and enliven new communities. This work has been created over the firm's fifteen short years and emerges from a design process devoted to a direct connection between architect, client, user and idea. Their immense variety of architectural experience empowers design that is fearless, yet purposeful. Ultimately, the buildings and spaces created are informed, unexpected, exciting and meaningful.

True partnerships are unique in a profession often too focused on star-architects and overwhelmed by international mega-firms. The partnership of Duda/Paine is founded in the duality inherent in a dedicated leadership of two that balances creativity with reality, innovation with discipline. This duality answers the needs of endeavors as diverse as healthcare and advertising, scales that span from small meditative projects to large corporate campuses, from arts education to financial institutions, and from focusing on healing and meditation to fostering interaction and engagement.

At its core, the Duda/Paine approach involves an unwavering commitment to the power of ideas and an equally insatiable appetite for idea generation. Every project within each of the book's five chapters represents their unique, genuine collaboration and their reverence for design, the business of architecture, their clients, their staff and each other. Throughout the volume is evidence of their collaboration's breadth, reach, sensitivity and beauty.

— Rebecca W. E. Edmunds

The book is organized in thematic chapters: Shaping Experience, Creating Context, Skyline Meets Streetscape, The Public Room and Transformations. Can you explain the thought behind the decision to use themes? What do these specific themes say about your work?

Jeffrey Paine   Our approach to design is based on ideas. And ideas are the core of our work and this book. None of our buildings look the same because we always go back to the idea. It might be a metaphor, such as the top of the Frost Bank Tower referencing the Yellow Rose of Texas or origami, or opening up views of the creative process of advertising through the design for McKinney's Branding Tower. This isn't something we invented, but it is something that Turan and I, on a very basic level, believe: that ideas and the experience of ideas inform our process.

Turan Duda   Yes, ideas are incredibly compelling in the process of design. The approach has to be about being completely open to new ideas while simultaneously following a very clear method of exploration. It seems a paradox to say we can be completely open to new ideas—ideas that can come from anywhere and anyone—and at the same time, follow a defined methodology of how to go about that exploration. It's not a free-for-all; it's not chaotic. It's an informed search for ideas. And I find those two qualities together to be exceptionally powerful.

Retrospection allows you to step back and look at your work in an objective way, and you can see what binds the work together. The artist Denzel Hurley was a college friend of mine. At graduation, I asked him, "What kind of work are you going to be doing?" I expected some theoretical statement about his work. And he said, "I'll let you know in 20 years." I find that such a profound statement. Because it's not until we actually engage in the doing, until we've done this for a long time, that ideas keep percolating to the surface. For Jeff and I, certain concepts keep recurring because we work from ideas and not style, building type or typology. At a certain point, we imagined we could layer these themes onto any project, but it quickly became evident that certain themes were stronger for each particular project.

JP   Building a body of work is also a way of self-exploration. We've recognized how we've come back to certain themes again and again. For example, the idea of public space, which speaks to a belief we have of blurring the distinction between public and private architecture. That's an important theme for the world today. So in practice, our process is informed by themes like the public room or the episodic experience of a building or space. In any great cathedral, there's an approach that is clearly trying to evoke an emotional response. A spiritual response. It has to do with how one sees the building from a distance, how one comprehends the building as one gets closer, and certainly as one enters the building and experiences it. There is clear and deliberate thought behind the architecture and the experience of the architecture.

You've worked on some of the most famous buildings and landmarks in the world, while you've also designed a number of smaller, more intimate scale projects. Are there differences in how you approach these differing project scales?

TD   In larger scale projects we establish a personal relationship with company leadership and typically try to understand their corporate culture from our relationship with that individual. In smaller projects, we often focus on the experience of someone who's going to be there. It also involves relationship, but a relationship of understanding the people who will ultimately be living, working, exploring or teaching in the space. In that sense, it's even more personal. It brings a secondary aspect to the work that is mission bound. Sometimes it's about defining a new paradigm. And that's a different kind of exploration.

JP   It's rewarding when we're involved with the people who are going to be the end-users of the building. At the opening gala for the Albert Eye Research Center at Duke University Medical Center, my wife and I sat with Dr. Fulton Wong. He'd been on the building committee, so I knew him and generally about his work. I asked him, "Tell me about your research." Well, he quickly left me behind because it got very scientific, but he began by saying, "My life goal is to cure blindness." Now, how can you not love being involved in anything like that? Providing a laboratory atmosphere, in a building that excites someone every day and maybe even spurs a quest to cure blindness? These buildings, whether they be medical buildings or laboratory buildings or theaters or libraries, they're very exciting projects to be involved in, because you feel like the thing you're creating has this purpose of being architecture with a context, but also there's these great things going on inside that somehow you have a small part in it.

TD   There's this duality: in large-scale we may not know who's going to inhabit the space, or who the ultimate tenants might be. It's more of a universal approach. In smaller scale projects we typically know the occupants, and it's much more customized in terms of thinking about how to make them work better, think better, create better. There's a much stronger social aspect to it. In one you're thinking about the social and in the other you're actually engaging in the social. You engage directly, whereas in the other, we can only imagine the impact. And in some cases, like with public rooms, we're instigating it. We're putting the right pieces in place to actually create that social interaction. It's not because a client actually asked us for public space in their program. We brought that social element to the equation, and it's been transformative for them.

Diagrams appear in every chapter, done both by hand and digitally. What do these say about how you work? Can you speak to the value of diagramming in architecture?

TD   The diagram is a vehicle for understanding and for creating a common language among a group of designers. But it's also a vehicle for communicating

the idea of a building by talking about its essence. That essence is critical, because it becomes the nucleus of a building's idea. A diagram encapsulates that idea and guides us in making decisions along the way and beyond. At every project phase, whether working with clients or working with young designers, from the most fundamental massing scheme to the last details of a building, it allows us to say, how does this reinforce our initial idea? How does it enrich it, or reinforce it or clarify it? It provides us a vehicle for making those decisions. It's a way of avoiding the kind of arbitrary choices that might otherwise be whimsical or frivolous. It's also part of our sense of rigor in establishing a disciplined decision-making process. But the diagram is also a way to show a client the essence of the idea that frames the conversation.

JP There's something very interesting in being able to convey—in a few strokes of the pen or pencil—the idea of the building. We create these diagrams, sometimes they're not even diagrams, they may be sketches you do after the building is complete. And you realize it's a way of revisiting: what thoughts were we putting together in the early stages of design and what led us to come to this building solution? There's a power in being able to diagram, in showing the initial thoughts that led to a solution.

You've mentioned concepts of creativity and rigor. Can you elaborate on this aspect of your work?

TD This is our science. Other fields have their own methodology and physical laws that define their work. There's a history and a theory to how all that comes to be. And ours involves a lot of analysis, looking at buildings and comparing buildings over the continuum of time. That analytical process dovetails into the notion of style being secondary. It gets to the question of how we go about innovating and creating in a way that is not purely based on an 'Aha!' moment, but rather through a process of discovery that comes from analysis and brings us somewhere we never could have predicted. These two elements come together using this methodology, and we say, that's a wonderful surprise. At the same time it's fulfilling something the client is looking for.

It's almost as though we're taking the narrative that we've been given by a client or the mission or the context, and simultaneously going through this intellectual, analytical process, and looking for connections, how do I infuse this process with this particular narrative? That's where the magic happens. It takes skill. It takes talent. It takes insight. It takes an ability to be inclusive, while at the same time being rigorous. And that's something that only comes with experience and solidifying the way we think and the way we process.

I'm fascinated with this notion of a process that is methodical and rigorous, but also yields its own magic that could never have been predicted. Frankly, we don't know when that 'Aha!' moment will be, because it may be in something we did a month ago. It might be something we learn from our client today that is more relevant to

work we did earlier. Because this notion of how am I connecting these two worlds to something that resonates, to something that echoes for them, to something that is essential, the process is ongoing. And it's always about getting to that essence.

JP We're very particular about this process and equipping people so they know what they're doing, not just from a design point of view. To see our people step up and do great things, whether it's excellent design or inherently knowing how to talk to a client about what we do, is inspiring. But it takes time. It requires commitment and discipline. And tremendous rigor. Rigor actually fosters creativity. It allows people to do their best work.

Cesar Pelli wrote the foreword to this volume. You both worked for Pelli, who is one of today's most influential living architects. How did that experience shape your approach to practice?

TD Cesar was Dean at Yale when I was a student there. At the end of one of his lectures, I asked him, "Who had the most profound influence on you and your work?" And he said, "Eero Saarinen." Of course I said, "But your work doesn't look anything like his." And he said, "Exactly. That's the point. What influenced me was Saarinen's process, how he thinks and creates architecture." As young designers, we look for people who have an affinity to the way we think and what we believe. I had a natural affinity for Cesar's process and recognize that his work is so idea based, yet it follows a very clear methodology. Jeff and I have taken that methodology further. First, our work isn't based on a single vision. It involves at the very least the two of us, but typically many others, which goes back to what we've said about how we practice and approach design.

JP Cesar's process of investigation and exploration was a great foundation for how we wanted to practice. For us, the idea of a working environment that is open yet rigorous brings confidence in what we do. We aren't afraid of the unknown, of not knowing what will happen next, because we have this breadth of experience and versatility in the work we do. It's incredibly freeing and informative for everyone involved. And I think it says a lot about how to create amazing architecture. It takes an awareness of people, which is part of what I love about practice. And the work becomes much more interesting. This view of architecture as a social art not only when it's complete, but in its creation is an amazing thing. We both understand and appreciate the social aspect of design on so many levels.

TD Another influence is more personal, it is about the kinds of questions to ask. The process of design involves intellect. So, we incite thinking and inquiry, analysis and awareness, but intrinsic to everything is a great sense of humanism: What will it be like to be in that place? How will it be moving through the space, touching the materials? What can be seen and what must be revealed? Cesar had this very clear, logical construct of how to make architecture, but underlying everything was

humanism and experience. That's profound, and it's what appeals to us in thinking about architecture.

After fifteen years, what makes this working dynamic strong enough that you not only share a workspace, but also actually sit at desks that face each other?

TD   Point counterpoint. Yin-yang. Opposites attract. But it starts with trust. We both have such a high level of respect for each other. We were able to see each other in another context. We worked together on projects for our last five years at the firm. So we got to see each other in battle, in front of our bosses, in front of clients, and working with other collaborators. If there's a better way of knowing someone's integrity, persona and modes of operating, I don't know what it is.

JP   It's one of those things that is so simple and clear. When we started working together over thirty years ago, we were, and remain, very comfortable in our roles. So this left-brain right-brain thing, there's a simplicity to it that people get. They understand it. Clients understand it. There's a real strength in how we work. This is a team sport. The way we have defined design is very much participatory. It's about getting people to do their best work, about inspiring them, and inspiring our clients.

1 SHAPING EXPERIENCE

As globalization and popular cultural dilute the uniqueness of place, it becomes increasingly essential that strong connections be established through the experience of built form. Architecture that explores visual, auditory and tactile perception anchors each individual's physical experience and intellectual understanding of their surroundings. Like storytellers, choreographers and filmmakers, designers can shape meaningful sequences of movement and discovery that add layers of sensory information, giving personal meaning to the architectural experience.

DUKE INTEGRATIVE MEDICINE
DUKE UNIVERSITY MEDICAL CENTER

DURHAM, NORTH CAROLINA

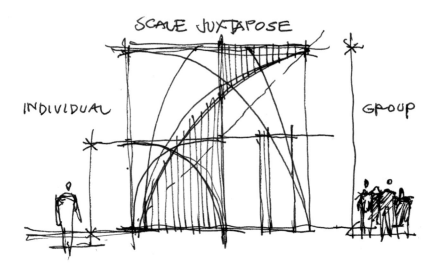

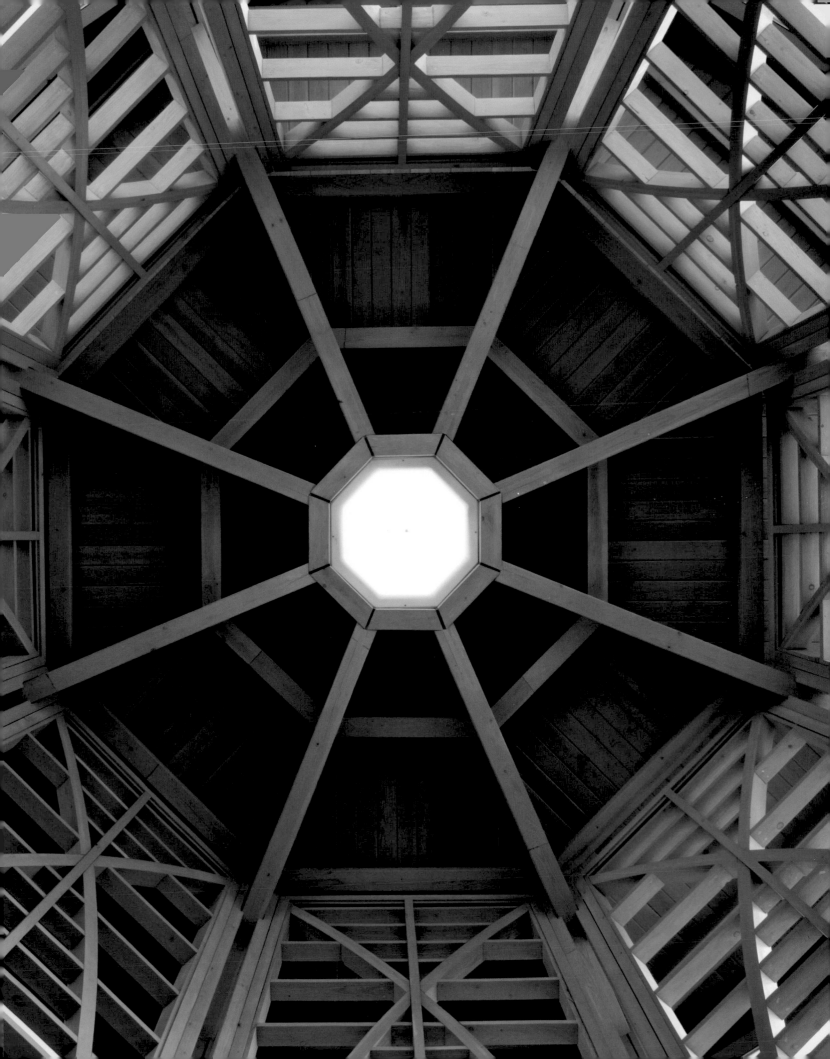

DISCOVERING PATHWAYS TO WELLNESS

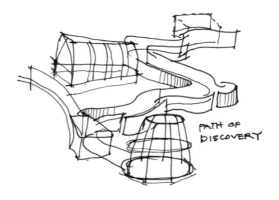

PATH OF DISCOVERY

Duke Integrative Medicine unites traditional, complimentary and alternative medicine into a new model of holistic healthcare for the mind, body and spirit. In addition to patients searching for a balanced and inclusive medical approach, the center serves healthcare professionals from many fields seeking a multi-disciplinary form of practice as well as community members interested in learning about wellness.

The design's linear, sequential and episodic circulation path blurs distinctions between interior and exterior, manmade and natural, reflecting the redefined boundaries that characterize integrative healing. Scale within the architecture varies between considering individual experience and the group dynamic required in today's treatment and wellness care. The form branches outward from behind a curving entry portico. Like interlocking fingers, its form projects toward the preserved Duke Forest while inviting the natural surrounding inside. Each path offers a different sequence of discoveries – meditative corners, framed views, gardens and fountains.

Two main waiting areas fully engage the senses: in the Tranquil Space, a garden and waterwall filter light and sound; in the Library, an overhead lattice inspires a visual meditation on structure and light. Changing textures underfoot draw attention to the physical act of walking. Views of nature throughout refocus patient and caregiver attention. Abundant natural light raises spirits. Varying textures of wood and bamboo impart warmth and welcome touch. When used structurally, as in the exterior canopies, the library and the central quiet room, laminated timbers mediate between built form and the surrounding forest. These elements come together to create a soothing environment that inspires and improves the healthcare experience.

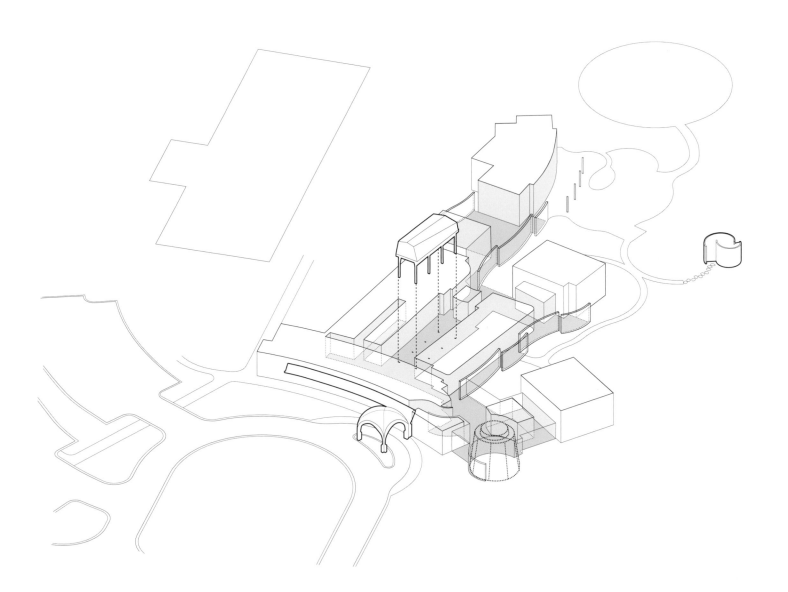

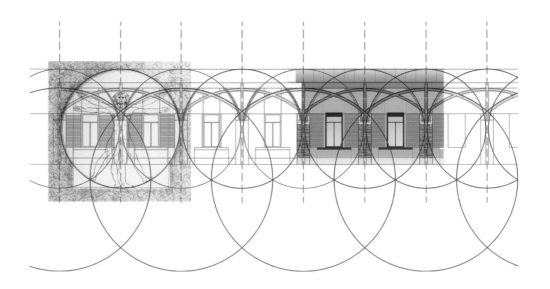

FORM FINDS INSPIRATION   The architecture acknowledges the integration of traditional and alternative medicine for mind, body and spirit.

BOUNDARIES REDEFINED   Clear distinctions between interior and exterior, manmade and nature echo the convergence of traditional and alternative modes of care.

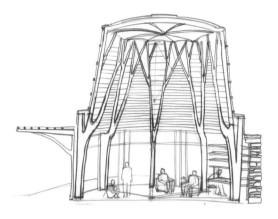

MELDING INSIDE AND OUTSIDE   Form and materiality coalesce to sooth and inspire occupants.

DREAM OF GREEN

DALIAN, CHINA

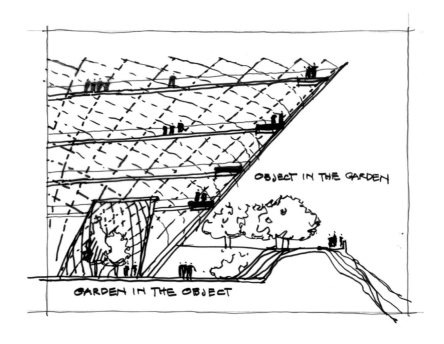

OBJECT IN THE GARDEN

GARDEN IN THE OBJECT

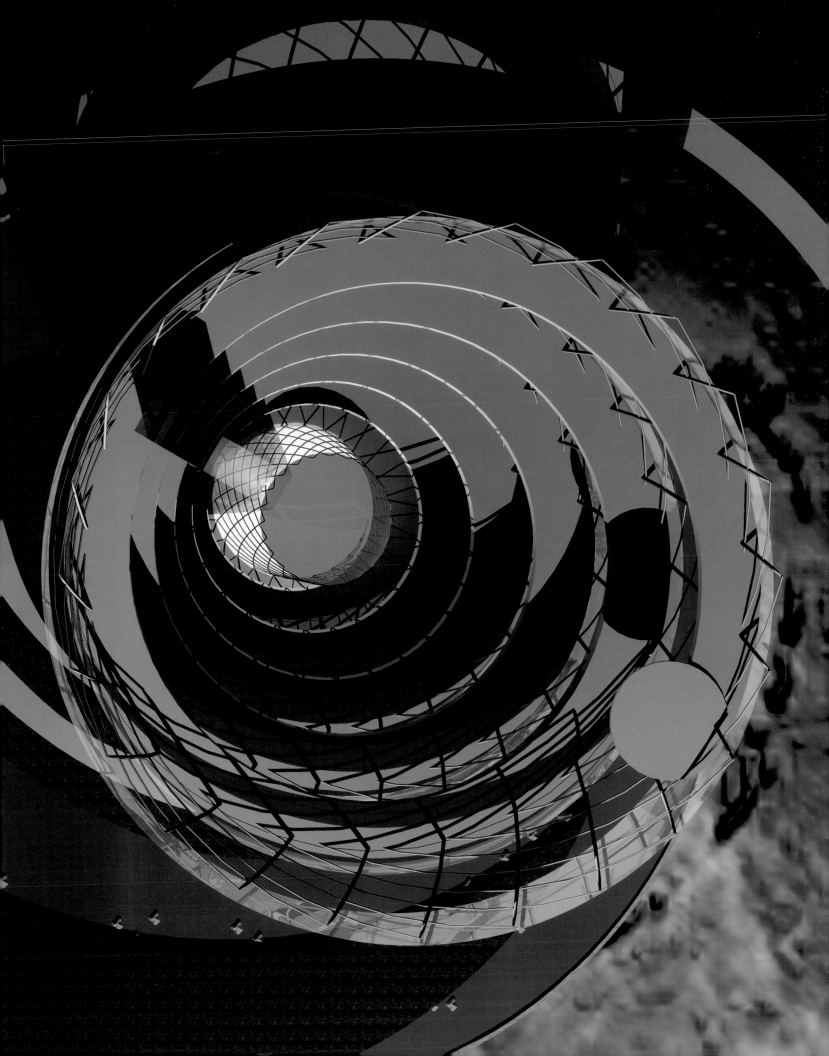

NATURE FROM WITHIN AND BEYOND

Tourism has become increasingly important to the city of Dalian, China, as it transforms into a major commercial center. The Dream of Green competition sought to transform a scenic overlook off a winding coastal highway into a focal point for a nearby state park with its extensive network of recreational trails. The solution explores the interconnectedness of man and nature with two intertwining spirals that represent the different realms.

The natural landscape and the built environment are experienced cinematically through movement in time and space. Movement along a spiral path is orchestrated through garden spaces, inspiring anticipation and emphasizing the path's three-dimensional central pavilion form. This choreography connects the site gardens, observation pavilion and elevated sea walk, while continually revealing distant views. Helical passage through the pavilion creates a continually shifting sense of space. Looking out to the sky imparts openness, while looking down into the structure creates a feeling of enclosure.

Visitors understand the project from the outside in – entering on foot from the gardens with the pavilion in the distance – or from inside out – approaching from the parking area directly into the Winter Garden. A site section illustrates the combination of different scales: the conical Observation Pavilion is embedded within the gardens; the enclosed Winter Garden rests inside the Pavilion's structure. This nesting of scales creates a paradox: a pavilion within a garden and a garden within a pavilion. Like Alice in Wonderland, one's sense of scale is continually altered. Shifting and varying views of the surroundings provide visitors unique perspectives on where they have been and where they are going, fostering a contemplative mindset for the citizenry of a country undergoing profound transformation.

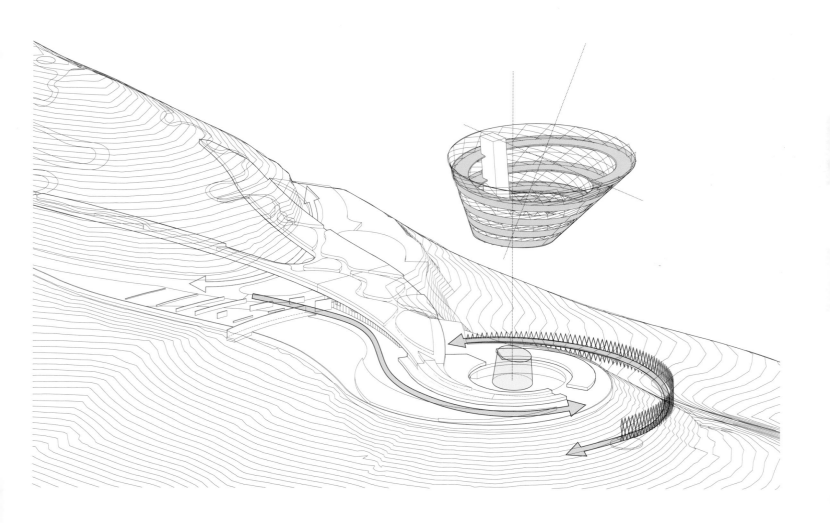

EXPERIENCING TIME AND SPACE   Movement is choreographed across the site through garden spaces, the observation pavilion and an elevated sea walk.

WELCOME CENTER
UNIVERSITY OF NORTH CAROLINA
SCHOOL OF THE ARTS

WINSTON-SALEM, NORTH CAROLINA

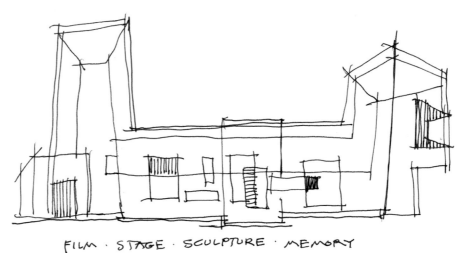

FILM · STAGE · SCULPTURE · MEMORY

REVEALING PURPOSE   The Welcome Center's purpose is unveiled in layers: first visually, as a lantern-like sculptural object, then physically, as a spatial volume, and finally intellectually, as a showcase for the school's seven arts disciplines.

XI'AN AEROSPACE MUSEUM

XI'AN, CHINA

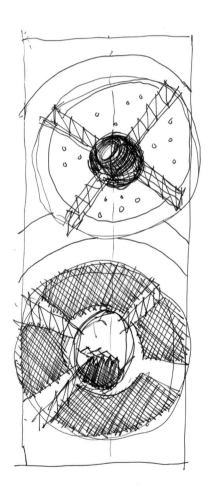

SHAPING DISCOVERY AND EXPLORATION

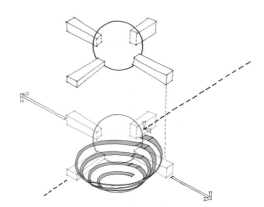

Within the past decades of China's unprecedented building boom, the 'wish lists' of developing cities have often included cultural institutions as metaphors for technological progress. The Xi'an Aerospace Museum celebrates the transformation of the ancient Chinese capital and terminus of the Silk Road into a progressive urban center.

Mankind's understanding of Space has developed in layered stages: with the eye, we have observed and formulated questions; with telescopes, we have gathered data, perceived patterns and made inferences; and with space travel, we've sent ourselves and our machines deeper into the universe. The Xi'an Aerospace Museum embodies this sequential, leapfrogging process of discovery – a spiraling cycle from visual perception to physical comprehension and back again.

The Museum's form is a planet-like, hollow sphere sliced at an angle and opened to the sky. The sphere's interior levels ascend from below grade, progressively revealing the layers of the atmosphere to visitors as they travel on orbit-like ramps around an inner void. This journey into space coincides with an exhibit on the timeline of space exploration. While each level exposes a new atmospheric layer, the subsequent chronicle of space exploration is also revealed. Artifacts, viewing instruments and interactive holograms illustrate the story of flight and space travel. The journey's final step brings visitors to the central Theater Orb – a cinematic showcase of new technologies. Thus, the museum experience culminates by suggesting the possibility and potential of future discovery.

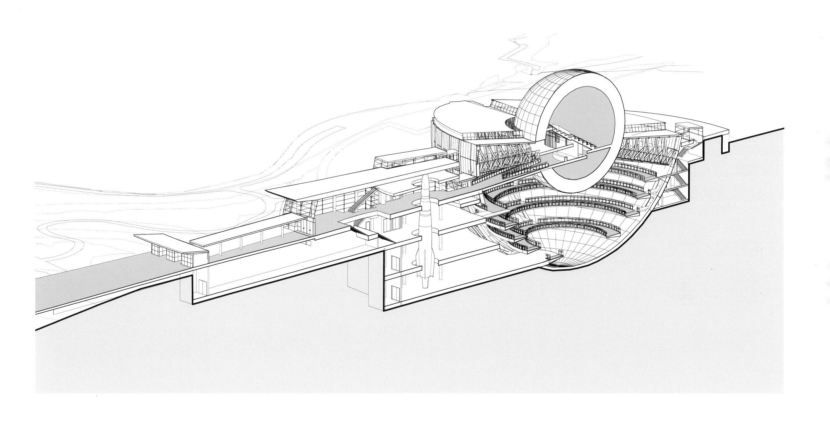

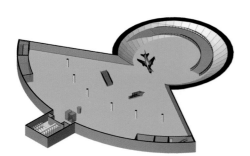
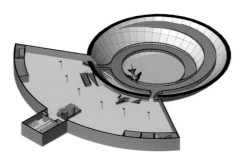
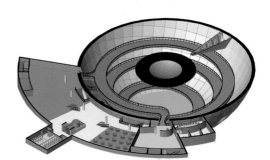

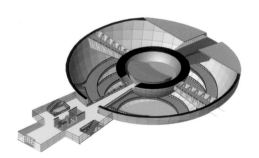

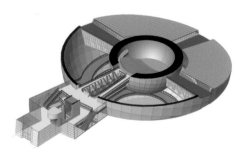

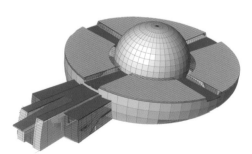

SHAPING THE EXPERIENCE

QUIET ROOM
DUKE CANCER CENTER
DUKE UNIVERSITY MEDICAL CENTER

DURHAM, NORTH CAROLINA

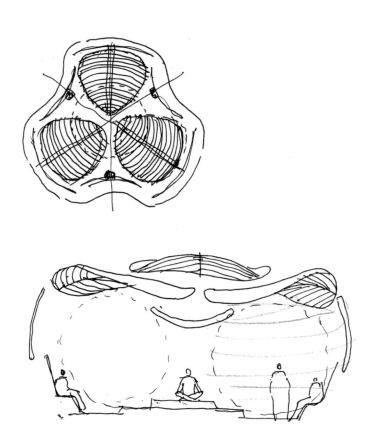

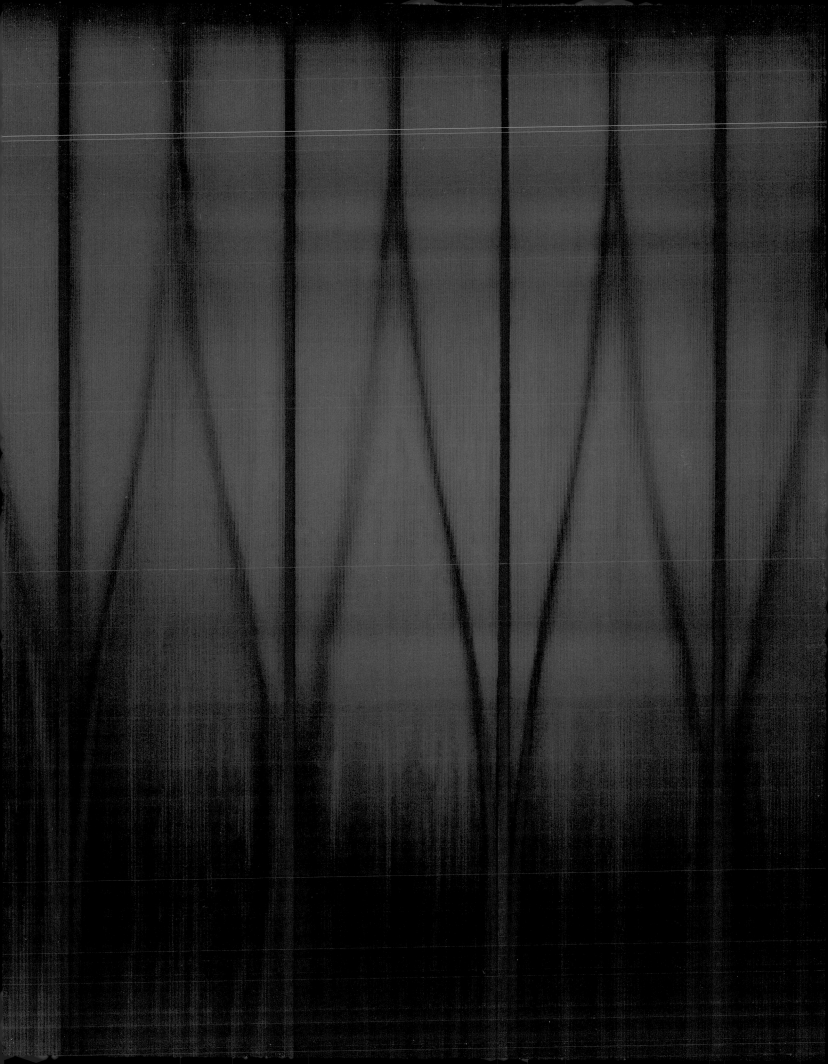

A CONTEMPLATIVE OASIS FOR CANCER CARE

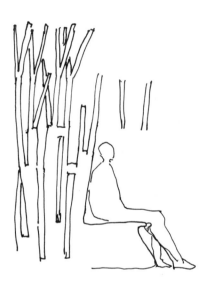

At Duke's new Comprehensive Cancer Center, patients, family and staff often face life-changing issues that bring differing emotional and physical needs. The Quiet Room's self-contained circular space is designed to address this spectrum of human experience through discovery and reflection. With simple references to nature and subtle manipulations of light and sound, the space provides a calming, meditative oasis amidst the Center's more institutional atmosphere.

The space's overall configuration creates three rooms within one. Labyrinth-like rings of paths, walls, seating and canopies encircle a glass fountain. The spaces within spaces allow for intimate moments, meditation, journaling, wandering, quietly conversing or joining a group for guided meditation or yoga. Discovery occurs through the combination and recombination of these fundamental elements. What results is personalized for the visitors, who each experience the sensual, visual and textural aspects of the space differently. By providing experiential and spatial alternatives, the Quiet Room accommodates a full spectrum of physical, spiritual and emotional needs.

Architectural strategies such as screening and translucence, apertures and lighting, layering and multiplication magnify a sense of spaciousness and inspire the imagination by fully engaging occupants' senses. Programmable LED lighting gradually shifts the room's ambient color and mood. Light seeps through the edges of recessed niches, washes the convex ceiling, and emanates from within the fountain. Reflections play off the stone mosaic floor's uneven surface and animate the room's inherent stillness. Subtly changing sounds mask background noise while providing a neutral atmosphere for contemplation or quiet conversation. Contrasting textures of wood, glass and fabric invite touch. The pattern, structure and craft of interior elements relate directly to the scale of the human body.

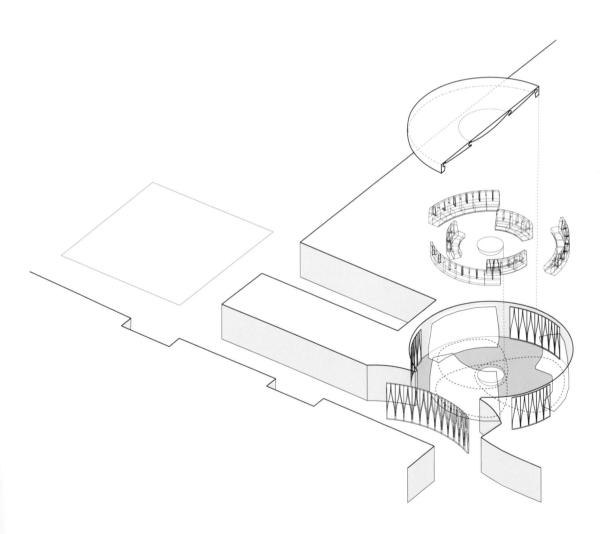

A Healing Space Designed To Nourish
Your Mind, Body, And Spirit

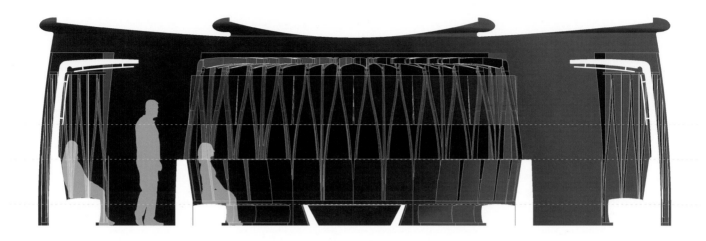

TRANSLUCENCY AND OPACITY   Transparent and impervious elements interplay to transform one room into three. Individual experiences arise from labyrinth-like paths that encircle calm spots of respite and a glowing glass fountain.

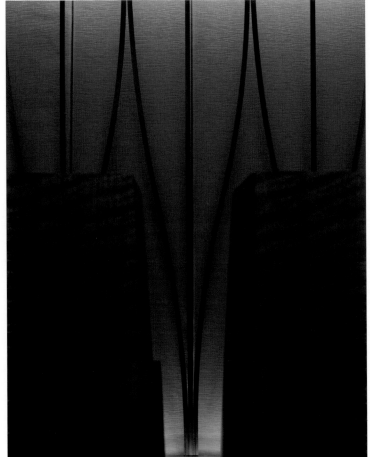

STILLNESS AND ANIMATION   Light plays through and across contrasting textures of wood, glass and fabric as color and sound shift, animating the room's inherent stillness and creating an atmosphere hospitable to the many emotions of cancer care.

2

CREATING CONTEXT

Design for suburban and city-edge settings often occurs in the absence of existing cues such as neighboring buildings, circulation paths and greenspace. Urban strategies can provide designers tools to create destinations where previously none existed. Each of the following projects looks to other forms of inspiration to create a unique sense of place. Using a balance of built form and open space, a contrast of manmade gardens with natural landscape, and the physical qualities of site and surroundings, these projects present new ways that architecture and place can be re-envisioned.

BLUECROSS BLUESHIELD OF TENNESSEE CAMPUS

CHATTANOOGA, TENNESSEE

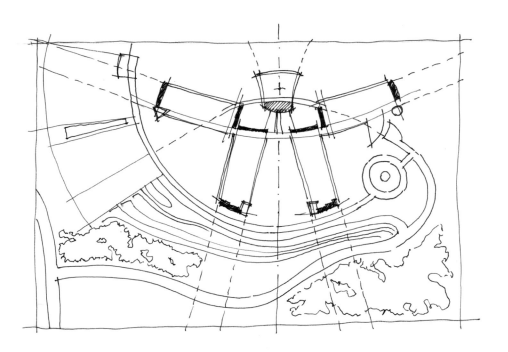

A HILLTOP CAMPUS EMBODIES SPIRIT OF WELLNESS

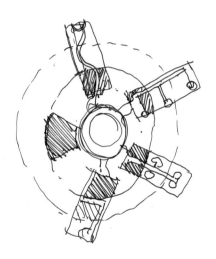

When BlueCross BlueShield of Tennessee decided to consolidate their operations into a single headquarters, they selected a prime hilltop location with panoramic views of Chattanooga, acres of undisturbed forest and direct access to the river. Overlooking downtown, the Cameron Hill Campus unites employees from ten previous locations throughout the city.

The campus embodies the company's identity as a knowledge-driven, wellness-focused organization. A key design theme centers on the organization's belief that physical and visual access to nature play a role in overall well being. Five buildings radiate outward from the crest of a hill, embracing a central plaza. This spoke-like array of buildings defines three interstitial garden spaces: a vegetable garden tended by employees; a forest with shaded pathways, seating and a pond; and a 'great lawn' for gatherings and outdoor events. For the buildings' occupants and visitors, these connective garden spaces become as essential as the buildings themselves. Translucent canopies unite the buildings around the central plaza and shelter a common promenade. Glazed walls throughout the complex create views across the campus' gardens and into adjacent spaces.

The hilltop site stands apart from downtown, yet the design maximizes visual associations and extends a network of physical connections to the community. The radial plan aligns with the city's grid and the central courtyard with downtown Chattanooga. The buildings fan out towards the city, a design strategy that reduces the complex's apparent scale through foreshortening. Public paths wind downhill through preserved forests to connect with the Riverwalk and downtown and reinforce the importance of a walkable environment for employees and visitors alike.

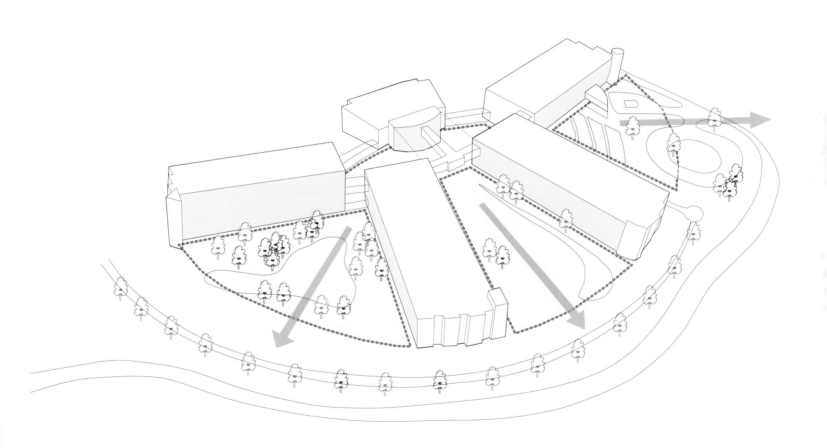

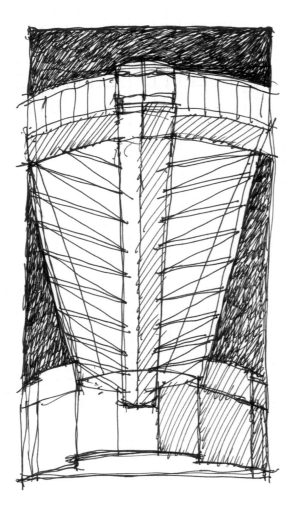

EXTENDING CONNECTIVITY   Expansive glazing allows views into adjacent buildings and across the campus gardens to the natural surroundings and community beyond.

COX CAMPUS AND GARDENS

ATLANTA, GEORGIA

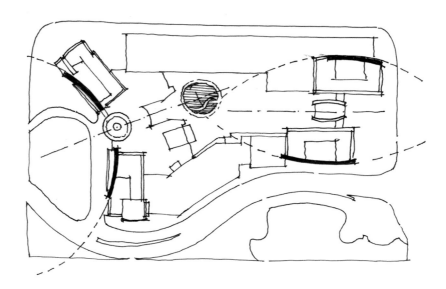

URBAN PARADIGM TRANSFORMED   Employee support and amenity spaces come together in a two-story commons building that anchors a central garden.

A NETWORK OF OUTDOOR ROOMS Terraced gardens and ponds form distinct spaces and provide numerous settings for employees to share ideas.

CREATING THE CONTEXT

TIME WARNER CABLE HEADQUARTERS

CHARLOTTE, NORTH CAROLINA

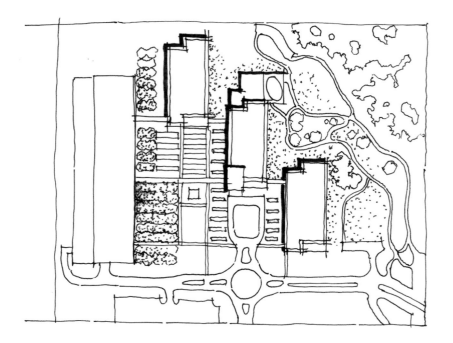

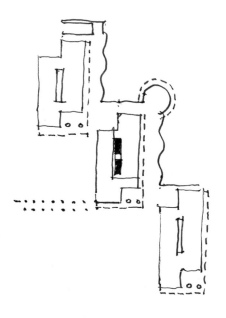

The Time Warner Cable Corporate Headquarters campus highlights the relationship between built form, manmade gardens and natural landscape. Thirty-five acres of open pasture, forest and wetlands comprised a lush natural setting, but lacked existing architectural context for the growing corporation. Instead the undeveloped sylvan site inspired design for expanded views of nature and the creation of a humane and sustainable working environment. Thus, the architecture of multiple buildings informs the landscape, creating a destination and shaping a strong sense of place.

Multiple buildings define the borders for a series of staggered formal gardens. Parking is placed to the side in favor of a garden forecourt with fountains, reflecting pools and walking paths that enliven the daily experience of arrival and departure. The gardens incorporate natural elements, creating a sense of transition between the manmade buildings and the organic world of undisturbed forests and wetlands beyond. A signature sense of place is expressed in the rich and subtle dialogue of the distinctions between man and nature.

The buildings stair-step on the site to ensure open views from all offices and reinforce the organization of the gardens. Their façades combine varying shades of spandrel glass to express the differing characteristics of built and natural landscapes. The elevation fronting the formal gardens features a rigorous grid that contrasts with the more playful, free form pattern facing the wetlands. This interplay between regular and seemingly random configurations conveys the essence of each realm – the rational, bounded gardens provide clarity and the native landscape beyond inspires inquiry.

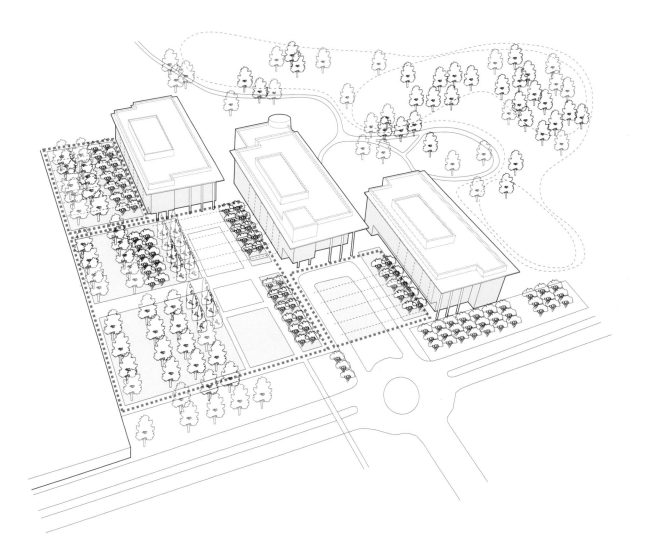

CREATING THE CONTEXT

TRANSITIONING NATURAL AND MANMADE   Across the campus, the architecture defines, borders and opens to a series of staggered formal gardens that reach out to the organic landscape beyond.

PALISADES WEST
DIMENSIONAL FUND ADVISORS
HEADQUARTERS

AUSTIN, TEXAS

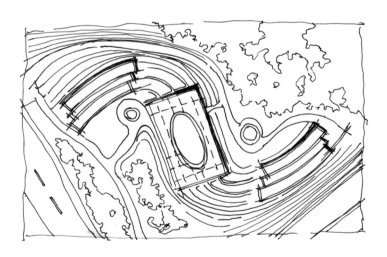

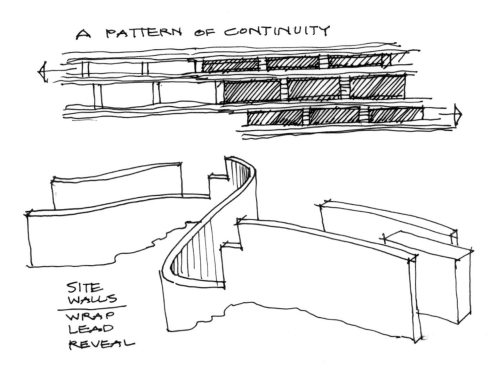

A PATTERN OF CONTINUITY

SITE
WALLS
WRAP
LEAD
REVEAL

ELEVATING GREENSPACE   A green roof garden covers parking for the campus' curved buildings, offering dramatic views and integrating architecture, gardens and surroundings.

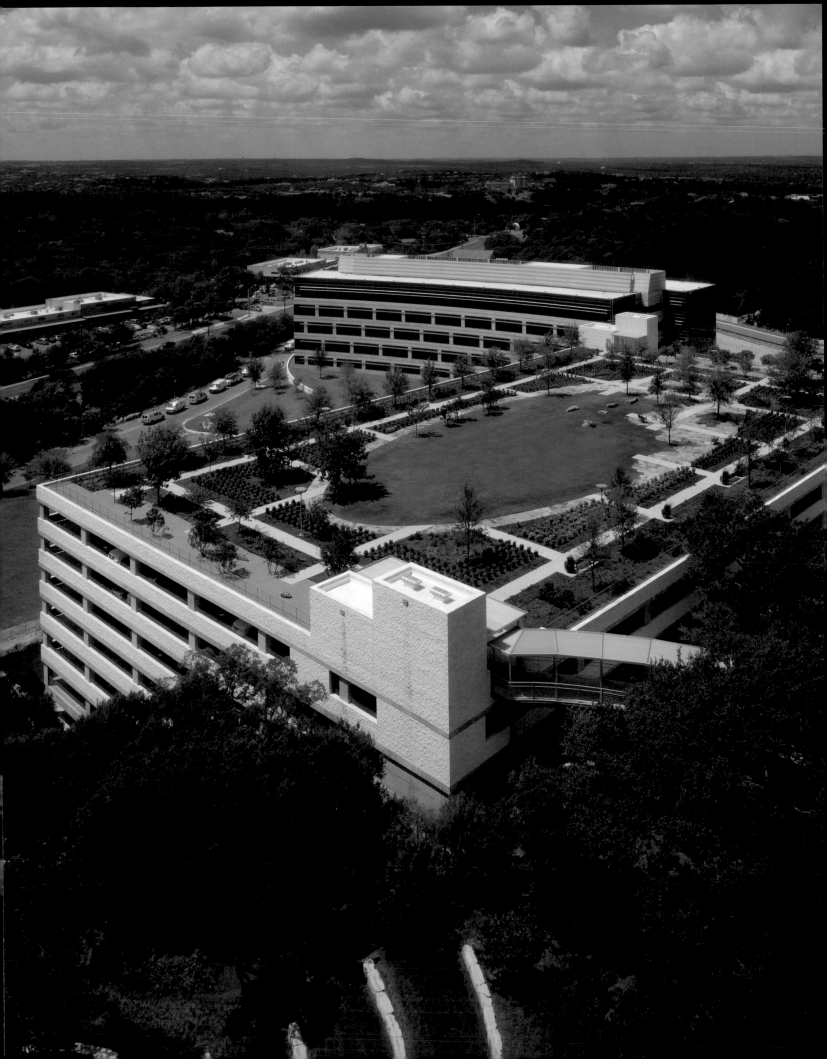

MIRRORING TOPOGRAPHY The building mirrors the site's geologic formation as plate tectonics inspire building elements to slide, bend, fold and break, shaping interior and exterior spaces.

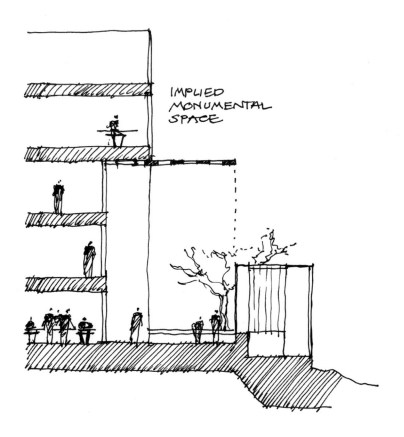

IMPLIED
MONUMENTAL
SPACE

'DATA IN STRATA'   Artwork by James Turrell in collaboration with Duda/Paine Architects.

EQUUS 333

MONTERREY, MEXICO

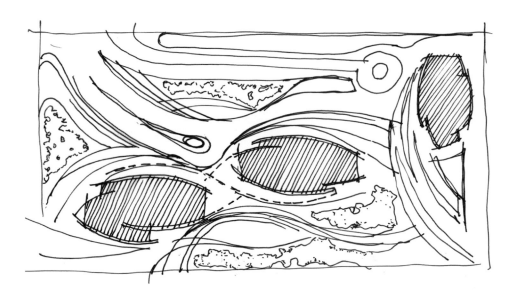

WHERE URBAN AND NATURE INTERSECT   Urban architectural form is juxtaposed against its surrounding natural landscape to reflect the dynamic interface that occurs when the two meet.

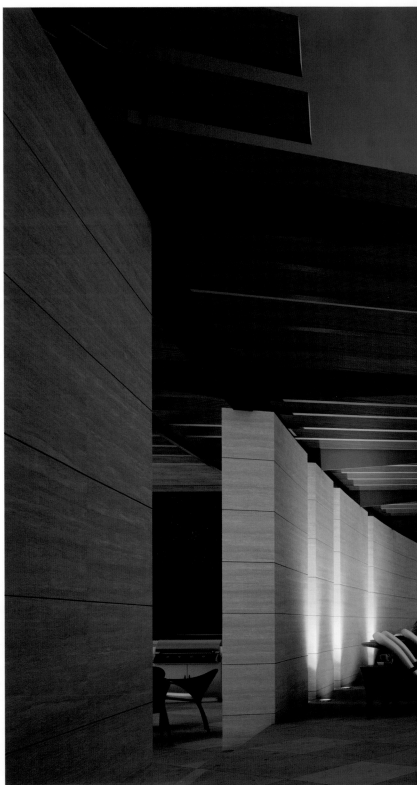

3

SKYLINE MEETS STREETSCAPE

For the first time in history, the majority of the world's population lives in cities, making the tower typology a crucial and consequential architectural form. Towers convey public gestures against the skyline and within the streetscape, acting at both the city scale and the more intimate scale of the human body. Whether seen from a distance or experienced close-up, these projects become landmarks in a city's skyline, simultaneously responding to characteristics of the existing urban fabric and amplifying the vibrancy of its street life, shaping a sense of expectation and anticipation for the city and the public.

FROST BANK TOWER

AUSTIN, TEXAS

SKYLINE MEETS STREETSCAPE

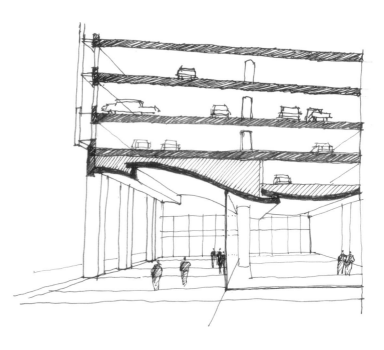

ORIGAMI OF GLASS AND STEEL   An origami-like crown of folded layers of glass and steel curtainwall create a memorable landmark in Austin's skyline. At night, its uppermost elements glow, transforming the crown into a beacon in the skyline.

PIER 1 IMPORTS HEADQUARTERS

FORT WORTH, TEXAS

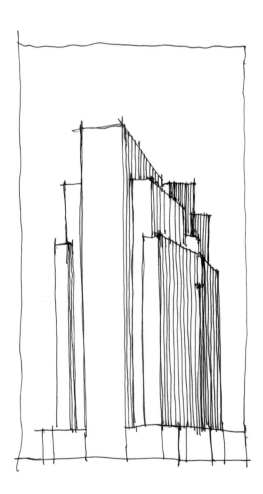

A LAYERED PROFILE DEFINES CITY'S EDGE

The broad-shouldered massing of the Pier 1 Imports Headquarters building responds to its panoramic setting, which lacked an orienting marker for the area's highest point. Visible from multiple vantage points near Forth Worth's central business district, the tower's beveled form becomes a sculpture-in-the-round, changing profile from broad to slender depending on one's viewpoint and angle of approach.

Surrounded by a lush, twelve-acre park at the edge of the Trinity River, the twenty-story tower forms the core for a development on the outer perimeter of the city. The approach winds through manmade gardens, encircling the building to arrive at a glass-walled, two-story lobby, which provides panoramic views of the surrounding grounds and functions as an event space for company and community gatherings.

The verticality of the building's layers of granite, aluminum and glass curtain wall draws the eye upward. The heavier granite at the base transitions to a glassy, lighter and more delicate form. The backlit, all-glass crest glows like a beacon at night, visible from miles around. The design reflects the relationship between skyline, tower, garden and river. Its shifting and layered silhouette enhances and engages the city's revitalized riverfront.

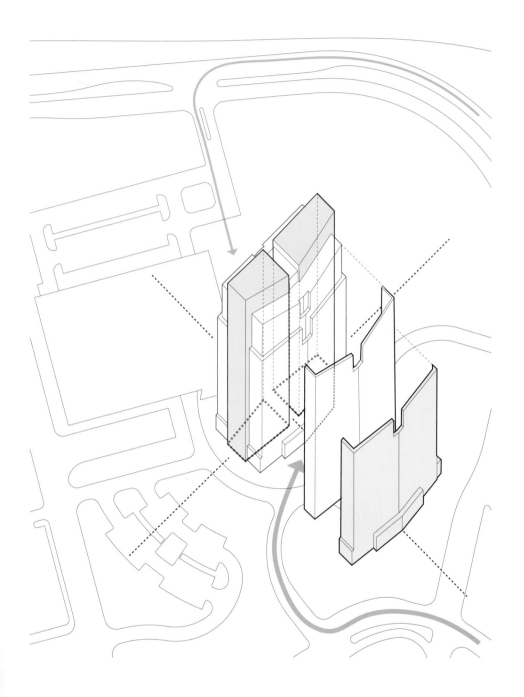

SHIFTING LANDMARK FORMS   The architecture's beveled massing is visible from downtown and major transportation routes. The building profile shifts from broad to slender depending on viewpoint and angle of approach.

SKYLINE MEETS STREETSCAPE

MAIN + GERVAIS OFFICE TOWER

COLUMBIA, SOUTH CAROLINA

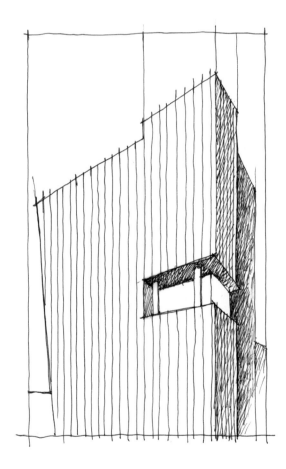

TRANSPARENCY AND REFLECTIVITY   A minimalist form of angled, asymmetrical, glass-clad façades strikes a subtle balance between transparency and reflectivity, suggesting the interplay between activity within the building and the surrounding city.

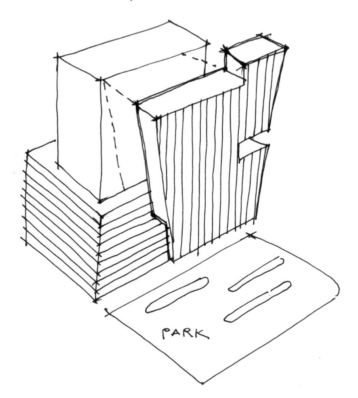

1221
MAIN ST

COLORADO TOWER

AUSTIN, TEXAS

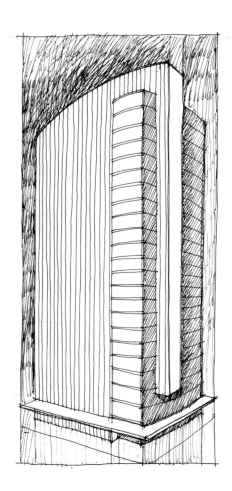

INTERLOCKING AND UNIFIED VOLUMES   Patterned and articulated glass
elevations unify the building's interlocking forms into a cohesive whole and at night
illuminate both skyline and streetscape.

601 MASSACHUSETTS AVENUE

WASHINGTON, DISTRICT OF COLUMBIA

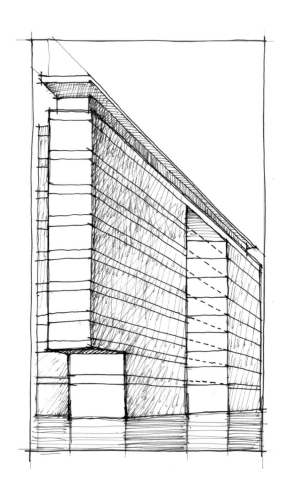

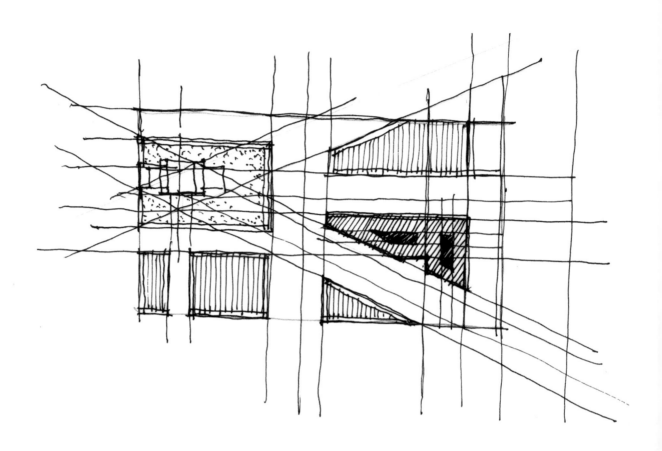

GEOMETRY AND UNIFORMITY   Façades shaped by site geometry and oblique intersections inform the eye-level urban perspective. Materiality differentiates building segments and a sense of scale along the 400-foot elevation.

SKYLINE MEETS STREETSCAPE

East Tower

TERMINUS

ATLANTA, GEORGIA

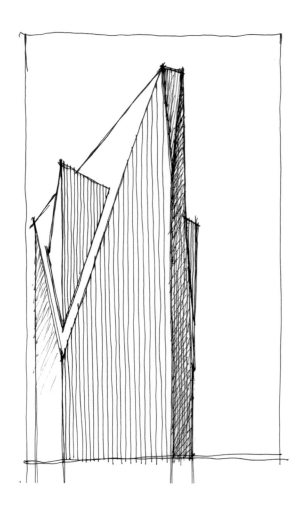

REDEFINING AND HUMANIZING URBAN DENSITY

The most successful towers incite multiple levels of experience, juxtaposing near and far, sky and ground. The chiseled and sculpted forms of Terminus occupy a full block in Atlanta's Buckhead district, creating a signature complex of distinct buildings that impact both the cityscape and the streetscape. Each of Terminus' three towers establishes a defined urban edge along Piedmont Street. They share a similar architectural language, yet each responds uniquely to its location within the site: Tower 100 accentuates the corner, Tower 200 marks the block's end, and a residential tower links the two. The design's ensemble approach shapes the dense clustering of towers that has become an Atlanta landmark.

Running parallel to the exterior urban edge, a protected internal street connects parking with shops, offices and residences. Here, employees, residents and visitors intermingle in shared public space. Pocket parks, roof gardens, and internal streets and plazas bring life to the street and create gathering places for community events.

Terminus contrasts sharply with surrounding low-rise, low-density strip malls and contributes positively to its urban neighborhood by generating pedestrian-level activity and commerce through public accessibility and reinforcement of the city grid. The project has attracted other high-density development to the area, shaping an environment where the mixture of living, working and playing leads to continuous day and night activity. Taller buildings, strong pedestrian orientation, easy access to public transportation, separation of pedestrian and automobile traffic, multiple open spaces, and a rich assortment of amenities all contribute to a compact, walkable environment.

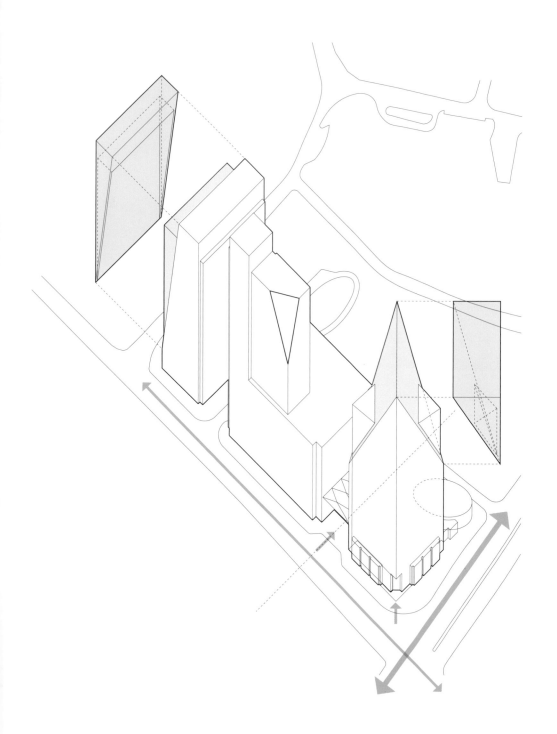

SKYLINE MEETS STREETSCAPE

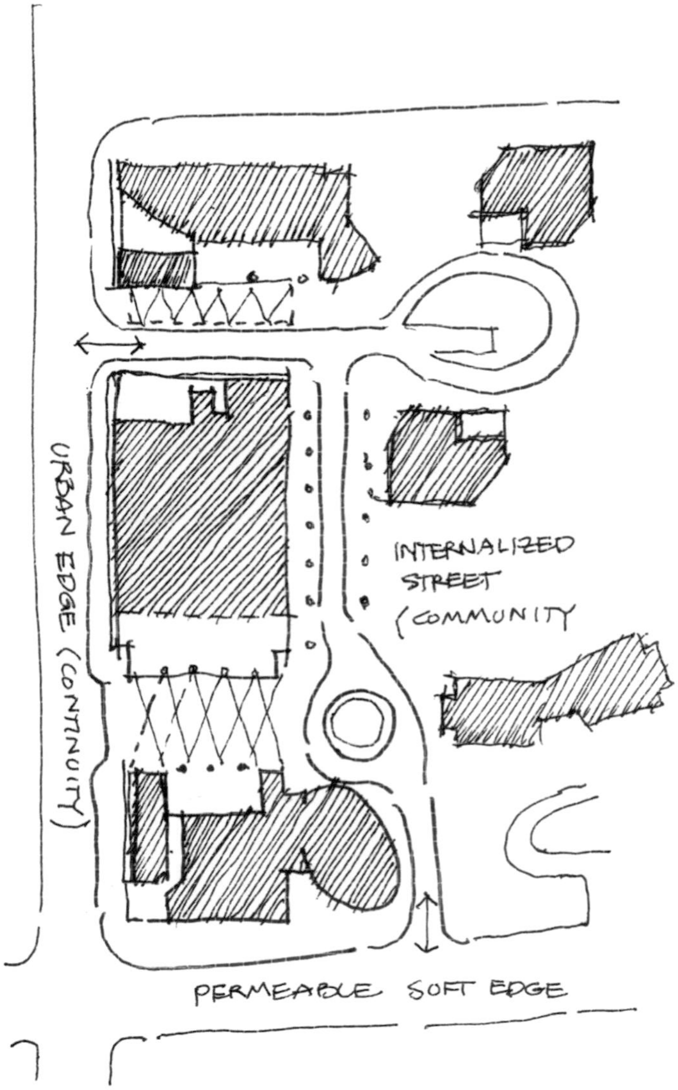
URBAN EDGE (CONTINUITY)
INTERNALIZED
STREET
(COMMUNITY
PERMEABLE SOFT EDGE

SCULPTING NEW URBAN EDGE The design's ensemble approach shapes the dense clustering of towers that is an Atlanta landmark.

SHAPING STREET-LEVEL EXPERIENCE   Pedestrian-level activity and commerce serve as sharp contrast to surrounding low-rise, low-density strip malls and contribute positively to the urban neighborhood.

4

THE PUBLIC ROOM

Shared experiences, collective memories and community connectedness remain valid and valuable counterpoints to today's hand-held, mobile and virtual social realm. Design's responsibility is to counteract the impulse that leads to gated domains and privacy screens, by providing public spaces that bring people together. Whether urban or suburban, indoors or out, public rooms nurture civic life by encouraging social interface through a sense of commonality that fosters chance encounters and casual interaction.

GATEWAY VILLAGE PROMENADE

CHARLOTTE, NORTH CAROLINA

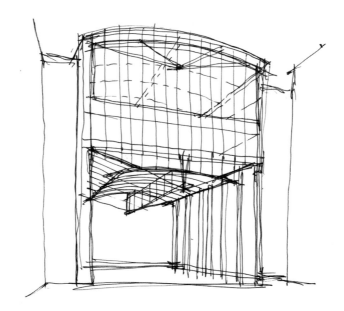

A NUCLEUS FOR NEIGHBORHOOD LIFE

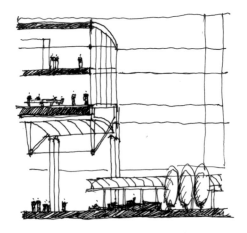

Privacy and security compel the design of forms that minimize, segregate and even eliminate consideration of public space. The vision for the Technology Center at Gateway Village included the rejuvenation of a neglected brownfield near the city center. The design turns the public/private dialogue inside out with the Center's 15-acre master plan, which is focused around a core of gardens, plazas, paths and open-air atria, and culminates in the Promenade – a large open courtyard, spanned by a double-level skybridge. This dynamic convergence of building form and open space addresses the confidential needs of the secured banking technology center within, while creating an open, inviting, highly accessible public space.

A promenade is a 'slow path,' not intended for quick passage, but for meandering, browsing and socializing. The Promenade is one element in a series of contrasting and differentiated outdoor spaces throughout the site. Choreographed movement along this sequence of spaces – from open to closed, light to dark, natural to paved – fully engages the senses to create a unique impression of place. This movement informs and illuminates the relationship between the buildings and open spaces, and how both accommodate and promote patterns of social behavior that contribute to a collective civic identity.

Gateway Village opens to embrace and enlighten future neighborhoods by defining civic spaces that reach out and connect beyond their boundaries. The complex has revitalized a formerly depressed area near Charlotte's downtown corridor, becoming a catalyst for growth and host to numerous public events within the Promenade. It has stimulated new development, a culinary-arts school and a round-the-clock, live-work-play environment.

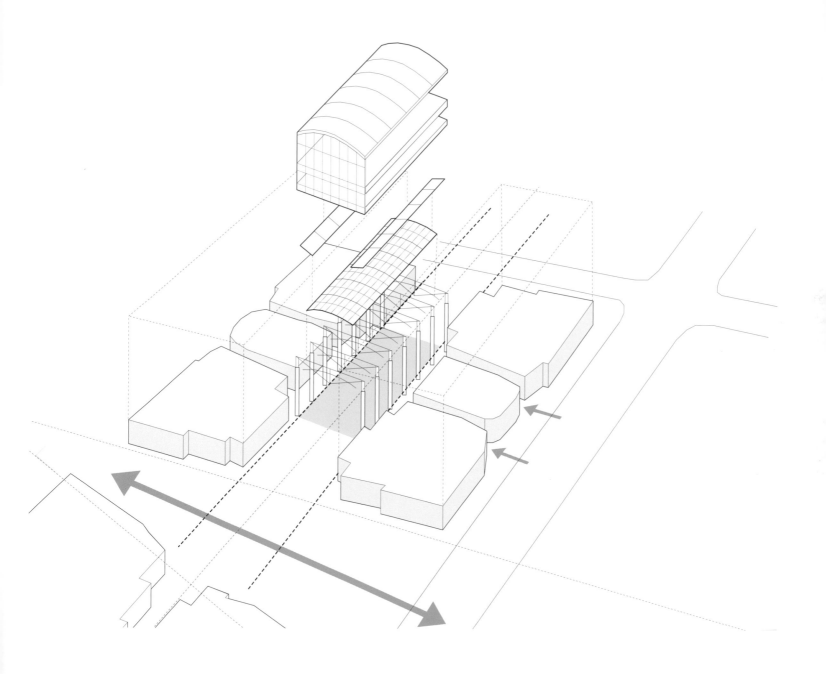

ENGAGING AND EXPRESSING COMMUNITY   Contrasting and differentiated outdoor areas inform and illuminate the relationship between buildings and open space and promote patterns of social behavior and collective civic identity.

CAFÉ STREET AT TERMINUS

ATLANTA, GEORGIA

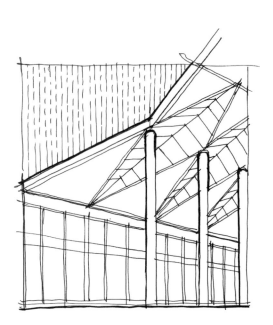

OVERLAPPING PUBLIC AND PRIVATE REALMS   The overlap of public and private spaces infuses energy and vitality, attracting other high-density development.

COX ROTUNDA

ATLANTA, GEORGIA

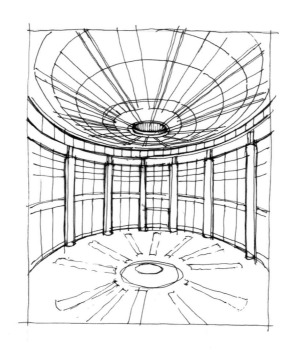

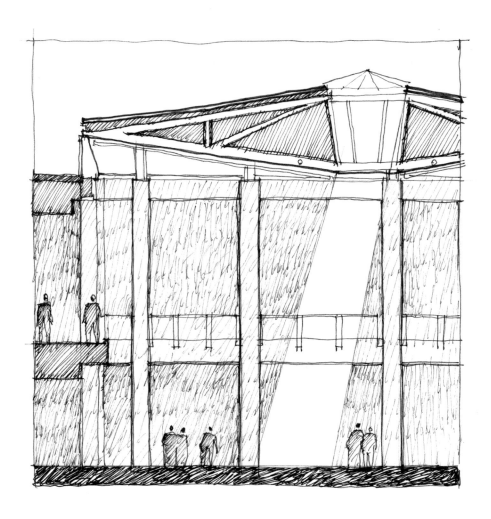

ROOM FOR LIVING   The Rotunda welcomes visitors while uniting multiple business divisions, becoming an unanticipated and valued venue for civic functions that strengthens company and community ties.

EQUUS 333 PAVILION

MONTERREY, MEXICO

A THRESHOLD BETWEEN WORLDS   Plaza and lobby merge to bridge multiple worlds: manmade and natural, private enclave and dense development, hard urban form and pristine landscape, and, ultimately, those of the two towers.

CTECH GARDEN PAVILION

ATLANTA, GEORGIA

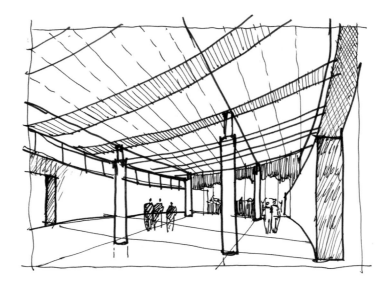

AN ORGANIZATIONAL CROSSROADS   Interlocking interior and exterior public spaces blur to impart continuity. Light filters through warm stone walls and a louvered wood ceiling, heightening occupants' awareness of the outdoors.

5

TRANSFORMATIONS

Progressive leaders in business, healthcare and education often aspire to cross disciplinary boundaries, collaborate more effectively and innovate more freely. They understand how architecture can realize the transformation prescribed in their visions of the future. In the complex interactions between architect, client, end users and community, the design process provides opportunities to realize new paradigms by bringing people together in ways that stimulate fresh ideas and practices. Ultimately architecture becomes the catalyst to redefine how we live, work, play and learn.

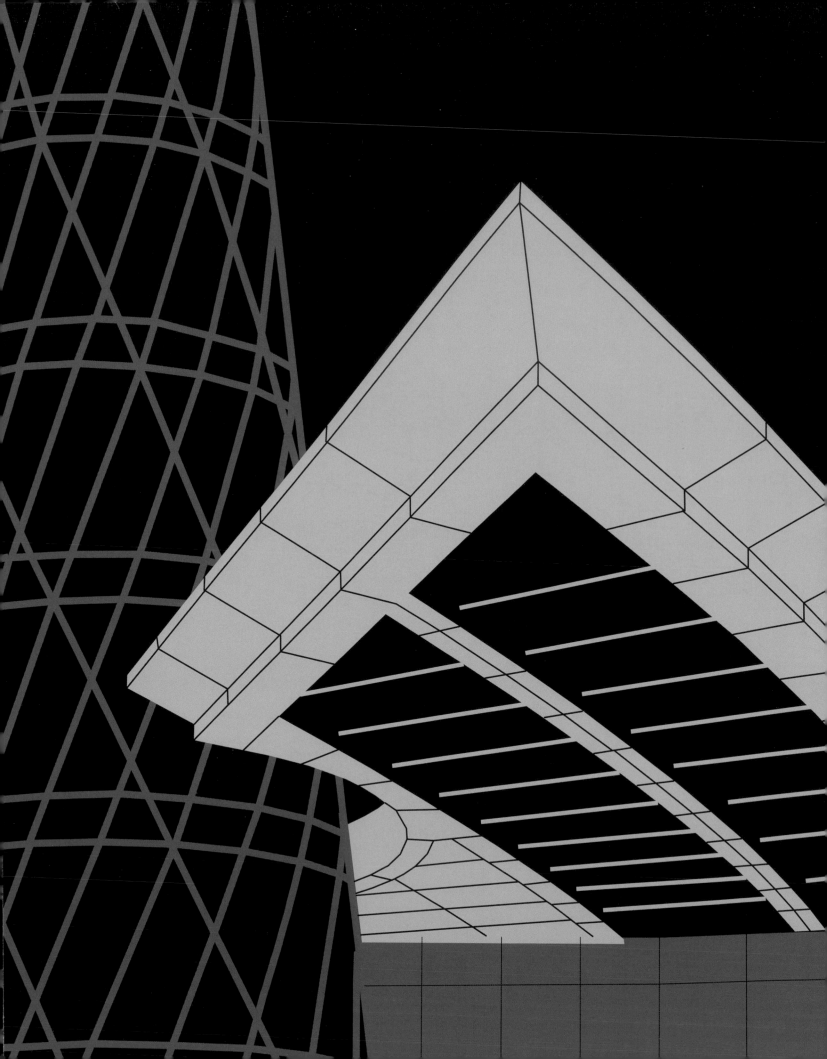

GATEWAY VILLAGE
TECHNOLOGY CENTER

CHARLOTTE, NORTH CAROLINA

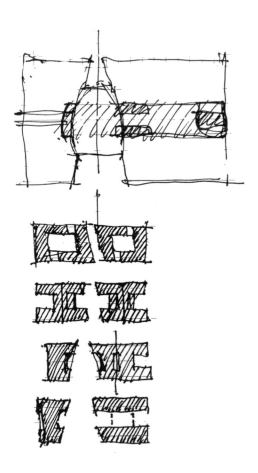

PUBLIC SPACE INSPIRES REVITALIZATION AND GROWTH

The master plan for the Technology Center at Gateway Village envisions a catalyst to revitalize a neglected area west of Charlotte's main downtown corridor. Located on reclaimed brownfields along a major entryway to the city's central business district, the project's centerpiece is the Technology Center, a complex of three office buildings with street-level shops, gardens and a courtyard promenade. To encourage downtown's transformation into a hub of live/work/play activity, the design provides for the 24-hour operations of a technology and call-center workforce around a vibrant, outdoor public space. A central core of gardens, plazas, paths and open-air atria throughout the fifteen-acre site connects housing units, offices, shops and parking.

The design creates an accessible, welcoming nucleus for urban village revival. Conceptualization began with a garden plaza core carved into the center of the complex, rather than the traditional approach of first considering the building architecture. Master planning concepts of scale, threshold and materiality redefine the site for its new purposes. The crisp detailing of the glass and metal façades of the Technology Center's buildings speak to the industry within while embracing the active public plaza. Seven-story modulated brick outer façades, deep setbacks and the arcaded pedestrian commons render the office buildings more compatible with the complex's residential neighborhood.

The most identifiable, and even symbolic, feature of the complex's design is in the purposeful overlap between public and private realms. Immense floor plates accommodate technology workers, while ground level public spaces seamlessly permeate and flow to the exterior. A double level skybridge accommodates highly secure workspaces by spanning and protecting the courtyard below. The complex has become one of Charlotte's most desirable locations for festivals, charity fundraisers and concerts. Gateway Village has also become the nucleus for new offices and apartments, as well as a renowned culinary institute. An underutilized site has been transformed to allow private enterprises to catalyze in a space that invigorates and revitalizes the public realm, embracing and facilitating future neighborhoods by defining civic spaces that reach out and connect beyond their boundaries.

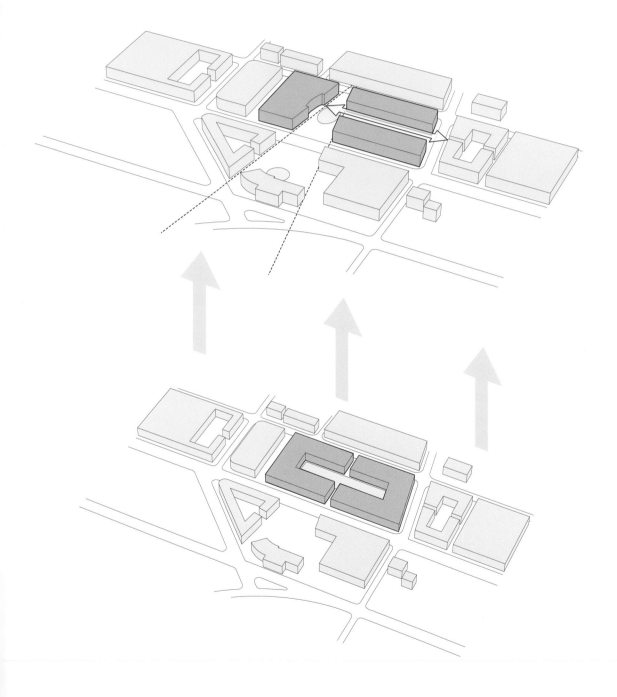

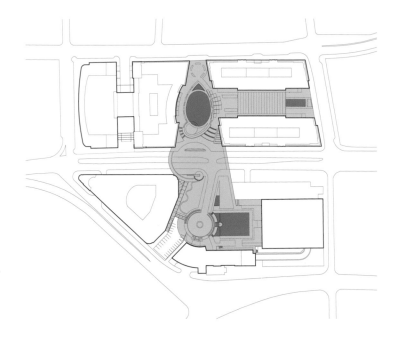

TRANSFORMATIONAL PUBLIC SPACE   A vibrant central core of gardens, plazas, paths and open-air atria throughout the fifteen-acre site connects housing units, offices, shops and parking.

VILLAGE NUCLEUS   The complex's central garden plaza utilizes scale, threshold and materiality to redefine the site for its new purposes.

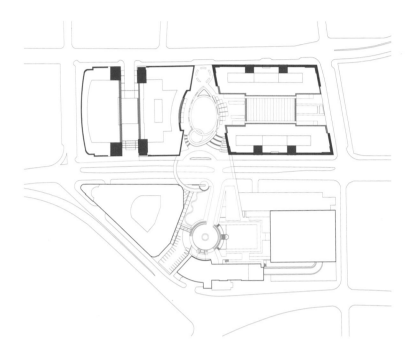

SPEAKING FROM WITHIN   Crisply detailed glass and metal façades speak to the industry within, while deep setbacks facilitate pedestrian activity and acknowledge the residential neighborhood.

McKINNEY

DURHAM, NORTH CAROLINA

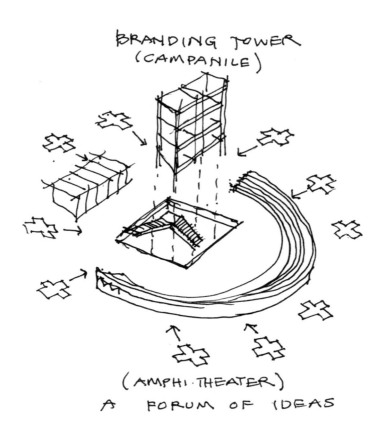

A WORKPLACE TO FOSTER INNOVATION AND CREATIVITY

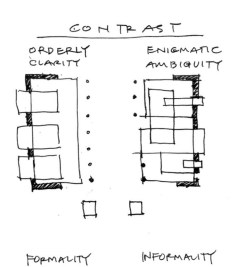

Digital and social media have revolutionized the advertising industry by placing a premium on collaboration across agency disciplines, particularly between left-brain analysts and right-brain creators. McKinney – one of a few top advertising agencies outside New York and Los Angeles – believed their physical environment could enhance idea generation. They often use biological terms – embryonic, incubation, gestation – to highlight both the vitality and fragility of the process in which a new idea is shared with progressively larger groups of collaborators.

The new McKinney Studio creates an urban microcosm within the shell of a rehabilitated tobacco warehouse that completely rethinks how the organization works. The path of an idea begins in the most private workspaces that line the periphery and ends in an array of gathering spaces that surround a central forum space, or amphitheater, which encircles a three-level 'branding tower.' Within the tower, account teams meet in 'brand rooms' to immerse themselves in their brand artifacts – products, sketches, storyboards, etc. – and stimulate the flow of ideas. Multiple roll-down screens can be continually reconfigured to show current ads or highlight activity within. Employees, who circulate around the brand tower many times each day, see other work in the office as clients catch glimpses of McKinney's creative engine at work. Surrounded by the central forum's hemicycle of seating, the tower provides the central stage and projection screen for 'town meetings' where fully developed ideas debut.

McKinney's new workspace has transformed the firm's level of collaboration and allowed their creative process to flourish. Touring the firm's office space demonstrates their unique working process to prospective clients and employees, making the space an invaluable marketing and recruitment tool. They credit the office design with the firm's accelerated leadership in digital and integrated communications, winning major accounts and becoming one of the thirty "Best Places to Work in Marketing" by Advertising Age in 2010. The White House chose McKinney's studio to host "The President's Council on Jobs and Competitiveness" in 2011.

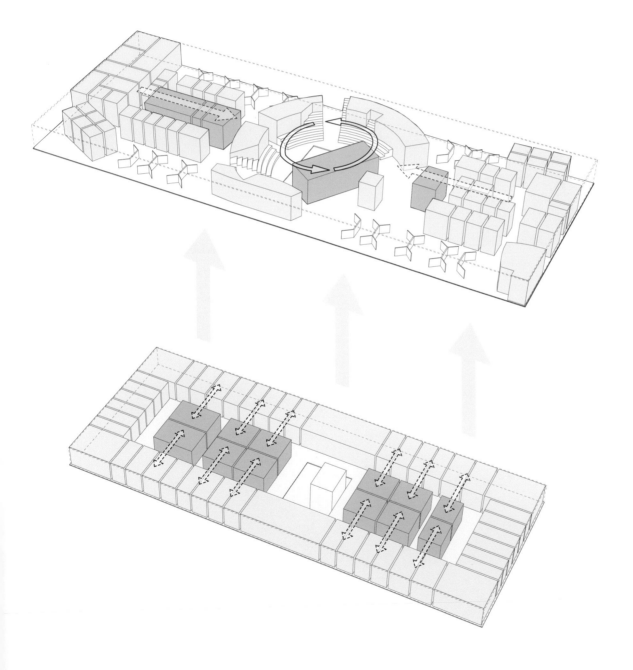

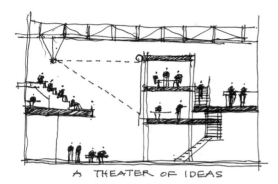

A THEATER OF IDEAS

SCHOOL OF PERFORMING ARTS
UNIVERSITY OF CENTRAL FLORIDA

ORLANDO, FLORIDA

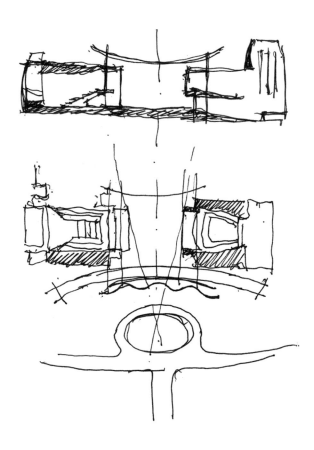

DISSOLVING BOUNDARIES   The performing and fine arts coexist in form and in the merging and overlap of teaching, performance, exhibit and common spaces.

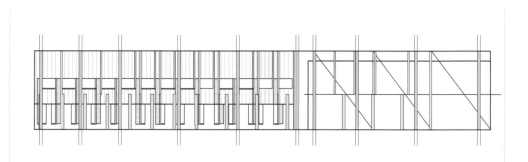

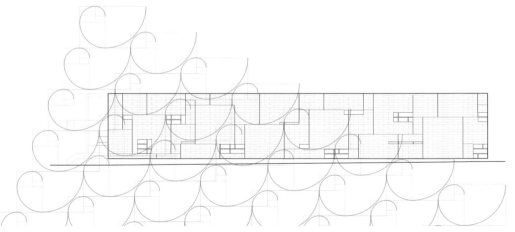

TALLEY STUDENT CENTER
NORTH CAROLINA STATE UNIVERSITY

RALEIGH, NORTH CAROLINA

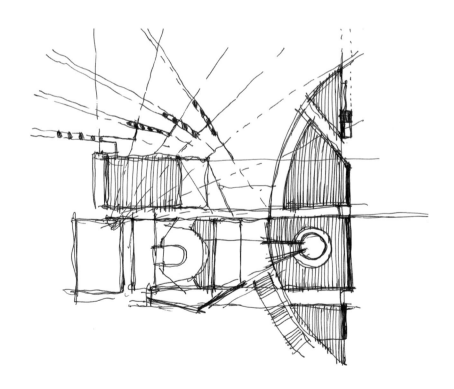

CENTER UNFOLDS TO CAPTURE STUDENT SPIRIT

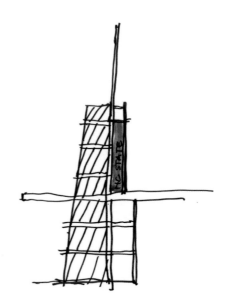

The Talley Student Center establishes a hub of activity that unifies and transforms the NC State University campus. This addition and renovation project creates a 'crossroad' – both literally and figuratively – that reflects and enhances today's intersection of traditional academic boundaries and social activity, as well as the integration of intellectual and social aspects of student life. Indoor and outdoor public spaces encourage interaction, fueling the creative energy that occurs when students connect.

Three primary knowledge domains within NC State University inspired the form and tectonic expression of the main parts of the building: a sweeping arc of transparent curtain wall with vertical glass fins characterizes the Technological Arts & Sciences; a monumental, central atrium with skylight creates a crossroad at the Center's heart signifying the Social Arts & Sciences; and the organic form, the light that filters through screens of terra-cotta louvers, and the direct relationship between interior dining spaces and exterior rain gardens captures the spirit of the Natural Arts & Sciences. The design's interplay of forms, materials and details embodies the increasingly interdisciplinary collaboration that characterizes higher education today.

Building massing opens the existing student center, reaching out to and unifying the campus. Interior spaces incorporate diverse programs across multiple levels, offering high visibility and a sense of identity for student organizations. In addition to its more traditional elements (performance spaces, dining, ballroom, and bookstore), the facility creates a student commons and establishes an iconic campus gateway. In contrast to the existing facility's introverted and impenetrable nature, the addition is a transformational and inviting welcome to students that shapes pedestrian circulation and links the campus' unconnected north and central areas. Each corner provides a campus landmark and orients students and visitors to the interior sequence of spaces. The Technology Tower marks the site's northeast corner and a future pedestrian bridge for North Campus.

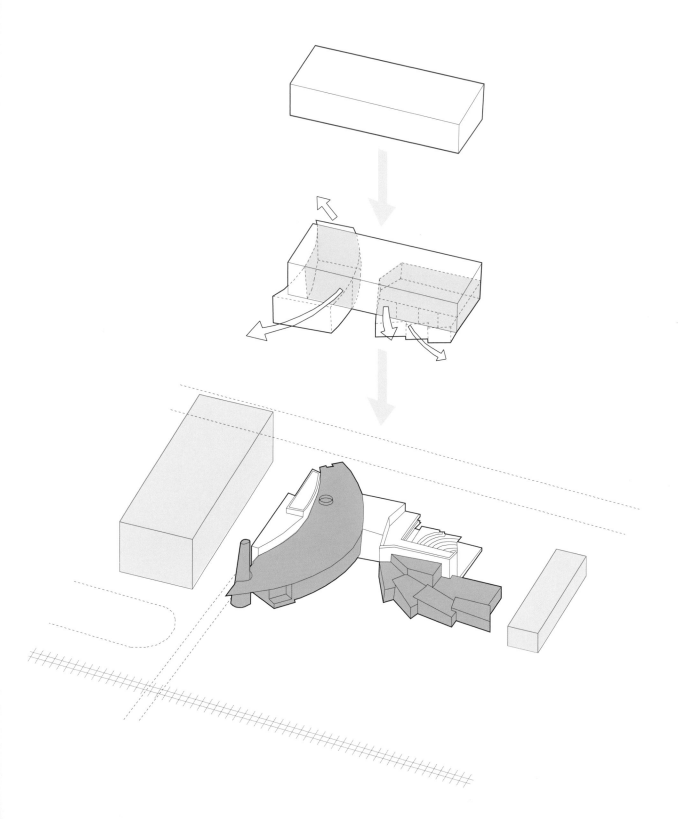

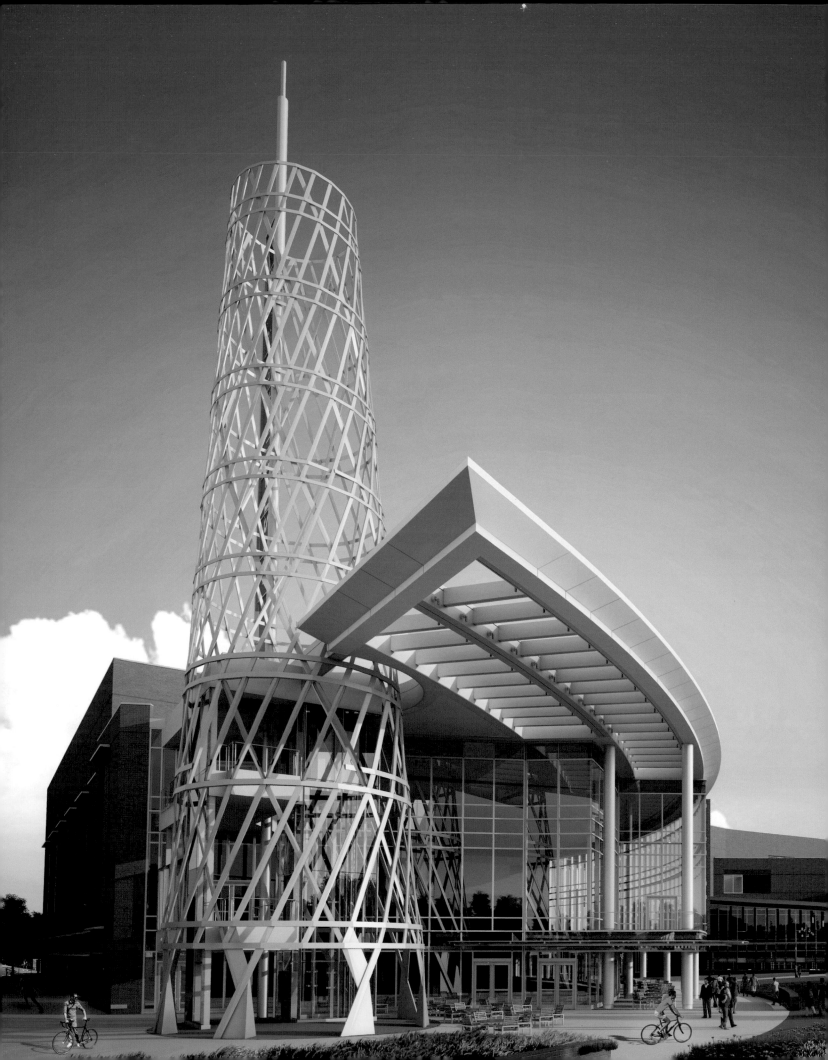

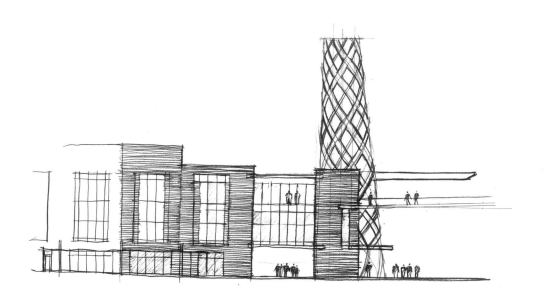

INTERDISCIPLINARY INTERPLAY   Higher education's increasingly interdisciplinary collaboration inspires the interplay of forms, materials and details, while public spaces foster interaction and fuel creative exchange.

JINZHOU NEW CITY MASTER PLAN

JINZHOU, CHINA

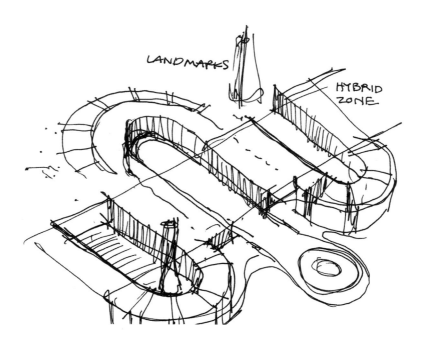

CITY-MAKING FOR THE CONTEMPORARY CONDITION

China envisions construction of 50 new cities over the next 20 years to accommodate over 40 million residents predicted to move from rural to urban areas. Global economics and resource demands ensure worldwide impact, posing either a tremendous environmental threat or presenting an unparalleled opportunity to marry urbanization with environmental stewardship. This provides the opportunity to create the world's first truly sustainable city.

The abstract interpretation of the very real and specific conditions of Jinzhou's waterfront site into a folded and compressed space yielded a conceptual city master plan that resembles three bends in a river. Each fold concentrates density and activity. The introverted western focal point channels water into itself, while its extroverted eastern counterpart projects out into the water. A central inland node relates to the water visually by framing a large, linear park that extends through the city's core to the shore. Variations in activity, scale and density among the three districts give each a distinct sense of identity.

This new urban paradigm preserves an essential quality of traditional Chinese urban planning. Although the proposal's rational order of grids, axes and central voids may appear formally driven from above, the pedestrian street experience differs dramatically. Such simultaneity of geometric order and experiential richness characterized historic Beijing – a formal structure that allowed the idiosyncrasies of everyday life, a harmonious balance between the perceived and experienced qualities of the built environment. Like slicing through folds, traversing the city presents the possibility for a richer passage: edges blur, activities overlap and zones intertwine. This exercise in 'tabula rasa' city-making offers a unique lens on how designers can condense the qualities of natural and incremental urban growth, which occur over many centuries, into the short timeframe of a master plan that charts the future of cities.

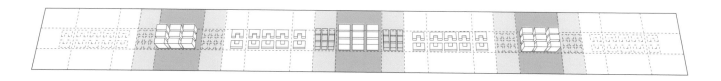

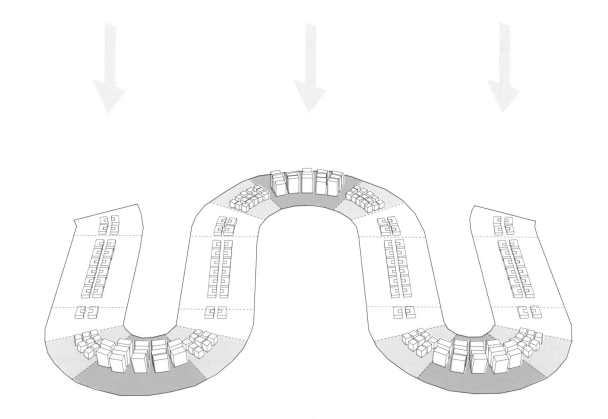

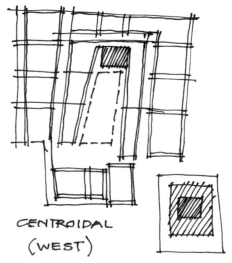

CENTROIDAL
(WEST)

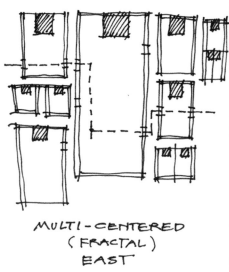

MULTI-CENTERED
(FRACTAL)
EAST

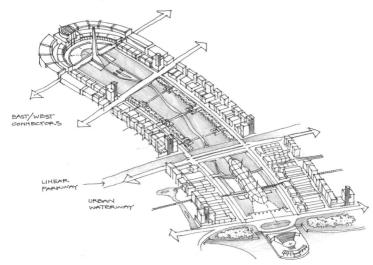

EAST/WEST
CONNECTORS

LINEAR
PARKWAY

URBAN
WATERWAY

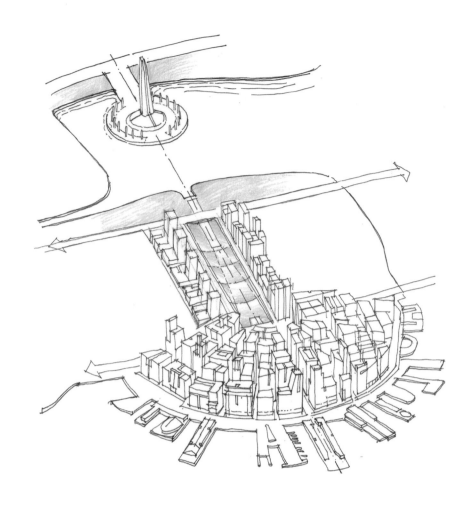

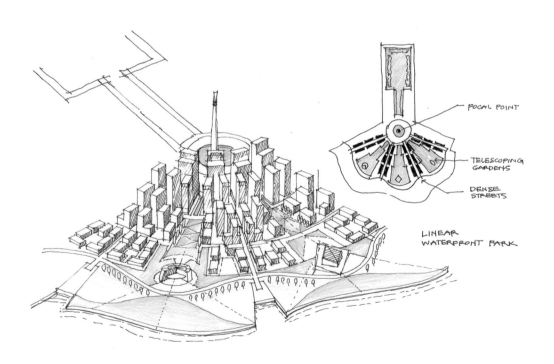

FOCAL POINT

TELESCOPING GARDENS

DENSE STREETS

LINEAR WATERFRONT PARK

TRENT SEMANS CENTER FOR HEALTH EDUCATION
DUKE UNIVERSITY SCHOOL OF MEDICINE

DURHAM, NORTH CAROLINA

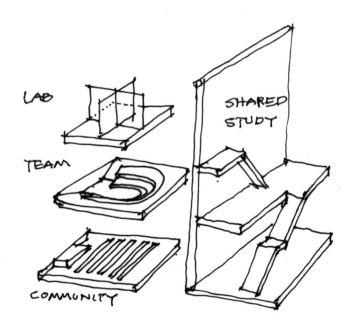

SHARED SPACES FOSTER A NEW PEDAGOGY

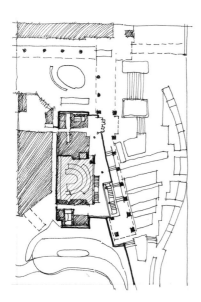

Tremendous advances in biomedical sciences and the increasingly complex role of the physician call for changes to education for future health care practitioners and leaders. Duke University Medical School has fully embraced a model in which students work together to solve clinical problems. This team-based learning approach relies on effective collaboration and communication. The new Center for Health Education design reflects this pedagogical shift and shapes an environment for it to flourish.

The Center for Health Education brings education to the heart of the medical campus – connecting it directly to the medical library with a short walk from Duke's hospitals, clinics, research facilities and School of Nursing. Ready access to nearby facilities strengthens relationships between research, education and practice. Increased contact between medical students, practitioners, researchers and educators, as well as students within the allied health professions, fosters communication and reshapes the educational experience. The building's transparency projects a sense of accessibility and connectedness to other medical disciplines on campus.

This new home for medical education also creates a second home for its students, dedicated equally to the academic and social aspects of learning. Teaching and learning spaces include a 400-seat auditorium, a Learning Hall with moveable configurations, flexible classrooms, dedicated study rooms and high-tech simulation laboratories that transform from mock clinical exam rooms to surgery suites and emergency rooms. As the hub of medical school community life, the fourth floor features a Student Life area with kitchen, TV area, lockers, meeting space and quiet zones. A generous rooftop terrace offers outdoor space for studying, relaxing and socializing.

Consolidating these formerly fragmented elements increases encounters and creates connections between students, residents, fellows, postdocs, faculty and staff. A rich array of gathering spaces promotes widespread collaboration, while centralized teaching and study spaces surround a three-story atrium. Small group rooms and open seating adapt to team discussions or individual study. Faculty offices dispersed throughout the building encourage informal interaction between faculty and students. For the first time at Duke, medical students from all four years can gather in one location for mutual sharing and learning.

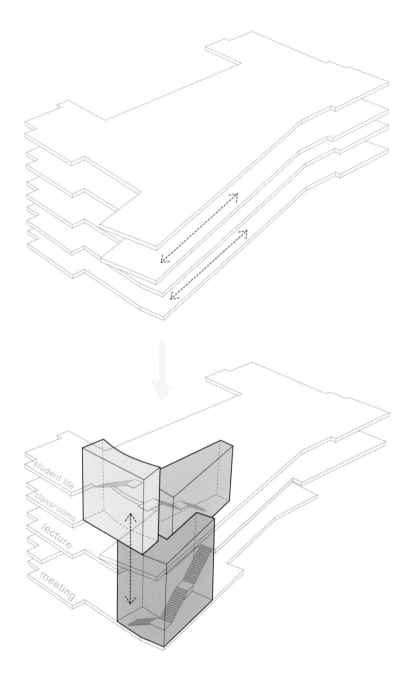

student life

classrooms

lecture

meeting

ENCOUNTERS AND CONNECTIONS   Gathering spaces are grouped and arranged to promote collaboration across formerly fragmented disciplines.

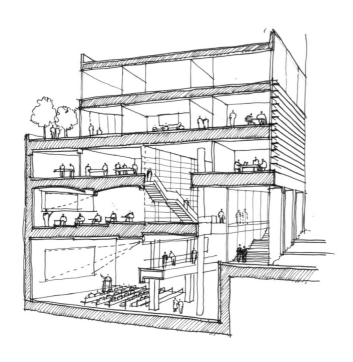

APPENDIX

DUDA/PAINE ARCHITECTS

Duda/Paine Architects is grounded in the dual forces of poetics and reality created by the long-established partnership of Turan Duda and Jeffrey Paine. These foundational concepts are woven together to create projects that are both great art and sound business. The firm's mission is to help clients realize objectives and transform their understanding and awareness of the value of spatial experience in shaping business, organizational and community success.

Duda/Paine's process is founded in discovery and involves achieving a highly nuanced understanding of their clients and the influences essential for organizations to thrive. The practice considers a diversity of typologies because it relies on methods of thinking and working that are transformative rather than prescriptive. Project design begins with identifying the essence of an organization's character and project purpose. This pre-design work helps clients refine their mission, and sometimes even alters their operations. What results is a 'spark' of invention and innovation that would not have happened otherwise. The firm's process bridges all project types, programs and markets, all scales and levels of complexity.

Duda/Paine is renowned for creating new paradigms for a diverse array of clients, who attest to the firm's ability to provide a detailed sense of project vision and purpose, while offering insight into the power of design and built form to shape and realize success. Duda/Paine Architects consistently brings intelligence and creativity to architecture, resulting in truly inspirational spaces for clients, users and communities.

STUDIO COLLABORATORS

Turan Duda
Jeffrey Paine

Russ Holcomb
Dave Davis
Sanjeev Patel
Scott Shell
Jay Smith
Brendan Beachler
Lynn Dunn
Darren Lathan
Treasure Lathan
Phil Lozier
Andres Serpa

Jorge Abad
Mollie Ackner
Leroy Ali-Osman
Khalid Almo
Ben Andrews
Manny Aretakis
Maria Avila
Amanda Badger
Scott Baltimore
Jane Bamford
Chris Bitsas
Andrew Blocha
Lisa Briggs
Mariana Brizuela
Dianne Brown
Amy Bullington
Craig Carbrey
Jason Carley
Michael Clapp
Jim Compton
Christina Conitizer
Craig Copeland
Tanya Cox
Amanda Cronick
Gary Farkas
Juan Filice
Pamela Fernandez
Stephanie Ferrante
Dougald Fountain
Scott Fowler

Megan Garrett
Frederick Givens
Edwin Harris
Brett Hautop
Marina Ilum
John Jennings
Mikhail Kim
Misato Kulpa
Melody Link
Allison Lowe
Ricardo Machado
Audra Marotta
Cecilia Martinic
Andrea McFarlane
Héctor Mendoza
Charles Menn
Emily Morgan
Ashley Morris
Nicholas Mshar
Andrew Nagle
Rodrigo Navarro
Joe Paradis
Matt Petr
Skye Pickholtz
Bethany Ratcliff
Silvia Raule
John Reese
Cassandra Rogers
Mandy Russell
Ryan Simmons
Dane Thompson
Lindsey Trogdon
Jesse Wetzel
Gillian Williams
Lisa Williams
Chad Wilkins
Marlen Veith
JoEllen Yeargen
Mao Yuling
Steve Zuber

CREDITS

DUKE INTEGRATIVE MEDICINE
DUKE UNIVERSITY MEDICAL CENTER
Durham, North Carolina
Client: Duke University Medical Center
Landscape Architect: HGOR
2003 – 2005
The 30,000 sq. ft. Duke Integrative Medicine center includes exam and therapeutic spaces, exercise and body-movement areas, a nutrition and demonstration kitchen, and faculty and administrative offices. The program seeks to address patient health needs through complementary and alternative medicine.
Design Team: Turan Duda, Jeff Paine, David Davis, Darren Lathan, Ted Givens, Jim Compton, Khalid Almo

DREAM OF GREEN
Dalian, China
Client: City of Dalian
Landscape Architect: HGOR
2008
This coastal landmark is perched on the cliffs southeast of Dalian overlooking the Yellow Sea. The garden pavilion features a conical spiral walkway culminating in a final 100' high overlook. The project includes landscaping integrated into the site along numerous walking paths, a cafe, souvenir shop and parking for 100 cars.
Design Team: Turan Duda, Jeff Paine, Darren Lathan, Phil Lozier, Manny Aretakis, Chris Bitsas

WELCOME CENTER
UNIVERSITY OF NORTH CAROLINA SCHOOL OF THE ARTS
Winston-Salem, North Carolina
Client: University of North Carolina School of the Arts
2001 – 2005
The 16,000 sq. ft. building to house visitor and student services functions and includes a media and encounter space to help orient potential students and their families to the school and its mission.
Design Team: Turan Duda, Jeff Paine, David Davis, Scott Shell, Darren Lathan, Ted Givens

XI'AN AEROSPACE MUSEUM
Xi'an, China
Client: City of Xi'an
2009 – 2010
The 10,000 m.2 Aerospace Museum is meant to be a central cultural venue for the City of Xi'an, exhibiting the history of aerospace technology in China. The program includes five levels of museum and a spherical 200-seat theatre-in-the-round, which appears to hover above the grand exhibit hall below.
Design Team: Turan Duda, Jeff Paine, Darren Lathan, Brendan Beachler, Phil Lozier, Mandy Russell, Chris Bitsas

QUIET ROOM
DUKE CANCER CENTER
DUKE UNIVERSITY MEDICAL CENTER
Durham, North Carolina
Client: Duke University Medical Center
2010 – 2012
The constraints of this 30'x'30'x11' interior space inspired an architectural strategy that seeks to alter the visitor's perceptions of containment by suggesting depth and light beyond. The contemplative space for one to fifteen people has a simple and profound intent: to be a calming and healing oasis for cancer patients and their families.
Design Team: Turan Duda, Jeff Paine, Chris Bitsas

BLUECROSS BLUESHIELD OF TENNESSEE CAMPUS
Chattanooga, Tennessee
Client: BlueCross BlueShield of Tennessee
Development Manager: Jones Lang LaSalle
Associate Architects: HKS, Inc. (Record)
TVS Design (Interiors), HGOR (Landscape)
2005 – 2009
Situated on top of a prominent hill overlooking downtown, the nearly 1,000,000 sq. ft. facility consists of four five-story office buildings and a fifth amenities building, all connected to one another by a series of sky bridges on the fourth floor. In addition to the all-open office environment, the program includes boardroom facilities, an employee cafeteria, fitness, training and conference facilities, health institute and a public welcome center.
Design Team: Turan Duda, Jeff Paine, Russ Holcomb, Jay Smith, Manny Aretakis, Craig Carbrey, Edwin Harris, Cecilia Martinic, Ashley Morris

COX CAMPUS AND GARDENS
Atlanta, Georgia
Client: Cox Enterprises, Inc.
Developer: Cousins Properties Incorporated
Associate Architects: HKS, Inc. (Record), HGOR (Landscape)
1998 – 2015
The central gardens for the Cox Companies are protected from the traffic and noise of the Perimeter Center area of Atlanta by the placement of the buildings housing office and amenity functions. The thereby internalized garden affords employees ample break-out and casual gathering space to encourage a sense of community. The program includes outdoor dining, lawns, wooded areas and water features.
Design Team: Turan Duda, Jeff Paine, Lynn Dunn, Craig Copeland, Sanjeev Patel, Phil Lozier, Héctor Mendoza, John Jennings, Dane Thompson, Manny Aretakis, Ben Andrews, Scott Fowler, Stephanie Ferrante, Ted Givens

TIME WARNER CABLE CAMPUS
Charlotte, North Carolina
Client: Time Warner Cable, Inc.
Development Manager: Jones Lang LaSalle
Landscape Architect: HGOR and ColeJenest & Stone
2004 – 2012
A three-phase development on a 50-acre suburban site, the corporate campus for 1,200 employees is unified through the use of interstitial gardens and walking paths. Structured parking for 1,000 cars, in lieu of surface parking surrounding the buildings, allows landscaping of these otherwise paved areas. Each of the three office buildings, constructed approximately two years apart from each other, range in size from 100,000 to 120,000 sq. ft. Campus amenities include a conference/training center, employee cafeteria, fitness center and lobby gallery highlighting the milestones in the company's history.
Design Team: Turan Duda, Jeff Paine, Russ Holcomb, Jay Smith, Lynn Dunn, Phil Lozier, Jane Bamford, Andrew Nagle, Manny Aretakis, Ted Givens, Ashley Morris, Rodrigo Navarro

PALISADES WEST
DIMENSIONAL FUND ADVISORS HEADQUARTERS
Austin, Texas
Client: Cousins Properties Incorporated
Associate Architect: Kendall/Heaton Associates, Inc. (Record)
2005 – 2007
Located on a sloped site overlooking downtown Austin, this two-building campus includes a 210,000 sq. ft. headquarters for Dimensional Fund Advisors, as well as a 160,000 sq. ft. commercial office building. The two are linked by an adjoining 1,400-car parking structure carved into the sloped site. A landscaped garden and sculpture pavilion sit atop the garage.
Design Team: Turan Duda, Jeff Paine, Chris Bitsas, Andrew Blocha, Amy Bullington, Jesse Wetzel

EQUUS 333
Monterrey, Mexico
Client: Legado Corporativo S.A. de C.V.
Associate Architects: Pladis / IP Proyectos (Record)
2011 – 2014
A 72,000 m2 urban mixed-use development on a 25,000 m. site. The program includes two office towers and a luxury condominium tower. The office towers rise 113 meters into the Monterrey skyline and create 360 degree views of the surrounding mountains. Each office floor plate differs in area due to the building's unique geometry. The 20-story condo tower has one residential unit per floor of 600 m2 each with varied amenities, including a pool on the lower levels.
Design Team: Turan Duda, Jeff Paine, Andres Serpa, Héctor Mendoza, Mandy Russell, Matt Petr, Ben Andrews, Diego Castilla, Jason Hines

FROST BANK TOWER

Austin, Texas
Client: Cousins Properties Incorporated
Associate Architects: HKS, Inc. (Record)
2000 – 2004
A 540,000 sq. ft. office tower and structured parking for 1,500 cars centrally located on Congress Avenue in downtown Austin. The program includes ground-level retail and restaurant with a covered public plaza for public events.
Design Team: Turan Duda, Jeff Paine, Lynn Dunn, Phil Lozier, Sanjeev Patel, Manny Aretakis, Mariana Brizuela, Rodrigo Navarro, Stephanie Ferrante

PIER 1 IMPORTS HEADQUARTERS

Fort Worth, Texas
Client: Pier 1 Imports
Developer: MBC / Dunn Consultants
Associate Architect: Kendall/Heaton Associates, Inc. (Record)
2002 – 2004
A 450,000 sq. ft. sq. ft. national headquarters facility that houses all corporate functions for this major retailer. The program includes a conference center, employee cafeteria, fitness center, photo studio, data center, sample room, and an 850-car parking garage.
Design Team: Turan Duda, Jeff Paine, Phil Lozier, Sanjeev Patel, Manny Aretakis, Mariana Brizuela, Chris Bitsas

MAIN + GERVAIS OFFICE TOWER

Columbia, South Carolina
Developer: Holder Properties
2007 – 2009
An 18-story, 200,000 sq. ft. office tower prominently located on the corner of Main and Gervais Streets in downtown Columbia overlooking the South Carolina State Capitol Building. The program includes a lobby-level branch bank, a signature restaurant with outdoor dining, a fitness center, and a 540-space, 6-level parking garage.
Design Team: Turan Duda, Jeff Paine, Russ Holcomb, Scott Shell, Andrew Nagle, Jorge Abad, Leroy Ali-Osman, Ricardo Machado

COLORADO TOWER

Austin, Texas
Client: Cousins Properties Incorporated
Associate Architect: Kendall/Heaton Associates, Inc. (Record)
2012 – 2014
A 650,000 sq. ft. 29-story office tower and 13 levels of above grade parking with 5,000 sq. ft. square feet of ground level retail space on an urban corner site in downtown Austin.
Design Team: Turan Duda, Jeff Paine, Jay Smith, Jane Bamford, Marina Illum, Dane Thompson

601 MASSACHUSETTS AVENUE

Washington, District of Columbia
Developer: Boston Properties, Inc.
2010 – 2015
This full-block 500,000 sq. ft. office headquarters building is adjacent to Mt. Vernon Square and features prominently along one of downtown Washington's busiest avenues. The dual core, L-shaped building, which follows the shape of the site while adhering to standard office lease depths, generated a building form that offers the added benefit of a large central, nine-story lobby atrium.
Design Team: Turan Duda, Jeff Paine, Dave Davis, Sanjeev Patel, Brendan Beachler, Ryan Simmons, Scott Shell, Ben Andrews, Allison Blanks

TERMINUS

Atlanta, Georgia
Client: Cousins Properties Incorporated
Associate Architects: HKS, Inc. (Record, Office), Cooper Carry (Record, Residential)
2004 – 2009
This large mixed-use development sits on the premier corner of Peachtree and Piedmont Streets in the heart of Buckhead in Atlanta and includes the 650,000 sq. ft. Terminus 100 and the 550,000 sq. ft. Terminus 200 office towers, a 200-unit condo tower and amenities deck, a large public gathering space known as Café Street, over 130,000 square feet of retail and restaurant space, and above and below grade parking for 3,500 cars.
Design Team: Turan Duda, Jeff Paine, Russ Holcomb, Lynn Dunn, Sanjeev Patel, Jay Smith, Andrew Nagle, Manny Aretakis, Leroy Ali-Osman, Chris Bitsas, Edwin Harris, Misato Kulpa, Silvia Raule, Jesse Wetzel

GATEWAY VILLAGE PROMENADE

Charlotte, North Carolina
Clients: Bank of America and Cousins Properties Incorporated
Associate Architect: Little Diversified Architecture (Record)
1998 – 2001
An architectural highlight of the Gateway Village mixed-use complex is a two-floor skybridge between two of the office buildings. Spanning 80 feet, the skybridge creates 100,000 sq. ft. of contiguous office spaces on two floors. Spanning above the sidewalk five stories in the air, the skybridge creates a soaring open-air public space below.
Design Team: Turan Duda, Jeff Paine, Lynn Dunn, Phil Lozier, Craig Copeland, Manny Aretakis, Maria Avila

CAFÉ STREET AT TERMINUS

Atlanta, Georgia
Client: Cousins Properties Incorporated
Associate Architect: HKS, Inc. (Record)
2004 – 2007
Café Street is the symbolic center and public events gateway into the Terminus mixed-use project in Buckhead. Open on both ends and flanked by the office tower lobby to one side and, on the other, a restaurant row on the ground floor of the parking structure, the large piazza is sheltered by a 60-foot high glass canopy above.
Design Team: Turan Duda, Jeff Paine, Russ Holcomb, Lynn Dunn, Jay Smith, Manny Aretakis, Chris Bitsas

COX ROTUNDA

Atlanta, Georgia
Client: Cox Enterprises, Inc.
Developer: Cousins Properties Incorporated
Associate Architect: HKS, Inc. (Record)
1998 – 2002
The Cox Rotunda grew out of the need for a single entry lobby for the Phase One and Phase Three Cox office towers, separated by over ten years in design. The space has become the central public meeting space for the company and hosts special events from black tie dinners to fund raisings and blood drives.
Design Team: Turan Duda, Jeff Paine, Lynn Dunn, Craig Copeland, Manny Aretakis, Scott Fowler, Stephanie Ferrante, Ted Givens

EQUUS 333 PAVILION

Monterrey, Mexico
Client: Legado Corporativo S.A. de C.V.
Associate Architects: Pladis / IP Proyectos (Record)
2011 – 2014
This canopied entry space hosts everyday and special events for either one or both office towers, with the view of the Sierra Madres mountains as a backdrop.
Design Team: Turan Duda, Jeff Paine, Andres Serpa, Héctor Mendoza, Mandy Russell, Matt Petr, Ben Andrews, Diego Castilla, Jason Hines

CTECH GARDEN PAVILION

Atlanta, Georgia
Client: Cox Enterprises, Inc.
Developer: Cousins Properties Incorporated
Associate Architect: HKS, Inc. (Record)
2010 – 2012
The second phase of the Cox Central Park Headquarters master plan includes a pair of 300,000 sq. ft. office buildings framing the northern edge of the internalized employee gardens. A louver-roofed garden pavilion serves as a satellite entry and employee connection for this state-of-the-art technology division.
Design Team: Turan Duda, Jeff Paine, Phil Lozier, Sanjeev Patel, Héctor Mendoza, Ben Andrews

GATEWAY VILLAGE TECHNOLOGY CENTER
Charlotte, North Carolina
Clients: Bank of America and
Cousins Properties Incorporated
Associate Architects: HKS, Inc. (Record- 900
Building), Little Diversified Architecture (Record 800
Building) ColeJenest & Stone (Landscape)
1998 – 2001
*This 1,200,000 sq. ft. mixed-use complex is located
along the entryway to Charlotte's central business
district. The program includes office and technology
center space for Bank of America and other users,
street-level retail and restaurant, a YMCA, and a
local radio station. Below-grade loading services the
multi-faced development.*
Design Team: Turan Duda, Jeff Paine, Lynn Dunn,
Craig Copeland, Phil Lozier, Manny Aretakis, Maria
Avila, Scott Baltimore, Ted Givens

MCKINNEY
Durham, North Carolina
Client: McKinney
Associate Architects: Alliance Architecture (Interiors)
2002 – 2004
*This 40,000 sq. ft. renovation of a tobacco warehouse
includes a three-story centralized conference room
'branding' tower with glass-faced conference rooms
and a 20'x 40' multimedia display.*
Design Team: Turan Duda, Jeff Paine, Ted Givens,
Gillian Williams

**SCHOOL OF PERFORMING ARTS UNIVERSITY OF
CENTRAL FLORIDA**
Orlando, Florida
Client: University of Central Florida
Associate Architect: HKS, Inc. (Record)
2007 – 2010
*Phase one of a multi-phased arts campus at the
University of Central Florida. This first phase includes
77,000 square feet of teaching and training facilities
for the theatre and music departments.*
Design Team: Turan Duda, Jeff Paine, Russ Holcomb,
Sanjeev Patel, Amanda Cronick, John Reese, Chris
Bitsas, Mikhail Kim, Jesse Wetzel

**TALLEY STUDENT CENTER
NORTH CAROLINA STATE UNIVERSITY**
Raleigh, North Carolina
Client: North Carolina State University
Associate Architect: Cooper Cary (Interiors) MHTN
Architects (Student Life Planner), ColeJenest & Stone
(Landscape)
2009 – 2014
*The Talley Student Center establishes a hub of
activity that unifies and transforms the campus. The
new 300,000 sq. ft. Center provides an additional
120,000 sq. ft. of space to the existing 170,000 sq.
ft. facility and will comprehensively renovate the
existing student center.*
Design Team: Turan Duda, Jeff Paine, Russ Holcomb,
Jay Smith, Scott Shell, Amanda Cronick, Andrew
Nagle, Joe Paradis, Mandy Russell, Chad Wilkins,
Chris Bitsas, Ricardo Machado, Emily Morgan

JINZHOU NEW CITY MASTER PLAN
Jinzhou, China
Client: Jinzhou Planning Bureau
2009
*Officials from Jinzhou requested a new vision for the
development of a future "whole city" which would
stimulate economic development through an urban
waterfront. The master plan suggests a hypothetical
future of increasing compression – in terms of both
time and function – and supports a new paradigm for
urban growth.*
Design Team: Turan Duda, Jeff Paine, Darren Lathan,
Phil Lozier, Ryan Simmons

**TRENT SEMANS CENTER FOR HEALTH
EDUCATION
DUKE SCHOOL OF MEDICINE**
Durham, North Carolina
Client: Duke University Medical Center
Associate Architect: The S/L/A/M Collaborative
(Record)
2009 – 2012
*The 80,000 sq. ft. education and social gathering
facility located in the heart of the Duke University
Medical Center Campus includes a consolidated
hub of student activity areas, a lecture hall and
conference center, classrooms and state-of-the-art
simulation labs.*
Design Team: Turan Duda, Jeff Paine, Scott Shell,
Andrew Nagle, Ryan Simmons, Ricardo Machado

PROJECT CHRONOLOGY

DIAMOND VIEW II
Durham, North Carolina
Capitol Broadcasting Company

DIAMOND VIEW I LOBBY
Durham, North Carolina
Capitol Broadcasting Company

AMERICAN TOBACCO MASTER PLAN, 1999
Durham, North Carolina
Capitol Broadcasting Company

GATEWAY VILLAGE TECHNOLOGY CENTER
Charlotte, North Carolina
Bank of America
Cousins Properties Incorporated

UNIVERSITY OF NORTH CAROLINA SCHOOL
OF THE ARTS MASTER PLAN
Winston-Salem, North Carolina
University of North Carolina School of the Arts

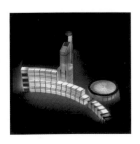

SHOWPLACE FURNITURE MART
Winston-Salem, North Carolina
Competition

TWO CORPORATE CENTER
Charlotte, North Carolina
Lincoln Harris

COX CORPORATE HEADQUARTERS
Atlanta, Georgia
Cox Enterprises, Inc.
Cousins Properties Incorporated

DUKE UNIVERSITY PERKINS PAVILION
Durham, North Carolina
Duke University

AMERICAN CANCER SOCIETY HEADQUARTERS
Atlanta, Georgia
American Cancer Society
Cousins Properties Incorporated

WELCOME CENTER, UNIVERSITY OF NORTH CAROLINA SCHOOL OF THE ARTS
Winston-Salem, North Carolina
University of North Carolina School of the Arts

FROST BANK TOWER
Austin, Texas
Cousins Properties Incorporated

PERIMETER CENTER MASTER PLAN
Atlanta, Georgia

ISLANDER BEACH CLUB AND RESORT
Ocean Isle, North Carolina

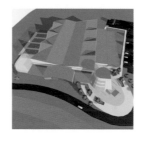

TENNIS TECH
Montreal, Canada

CHAPEL HILL GATEWAY MASTER PLAN
Chapel Hill, North Carolina

DUKE NORTH COVERED WALKWAY
Durham, North Carolina
Duke University Medical Center

DOWNTOWN RICHMOND MASTER PLAN
Richmond, Virginia

VICTORY PARK TOWER
Dallas, Texas
Cousins Properties Incorporated

WEST END CHARLOTTE MASTER PLAN
Charlotte, North Carolina
The Crosland Group

FIRST CITIZENS BANK HEADQUARTERS
Columbia, South Carolina
First Citizens Bank

ALBERT EYE RESEARCH INSTITUTE
DUKE UNIVERSITY MEDICAL CENTER
Durham, North Carolina
Duke University Medical Center

TIME WARNER CABLE CAMPUS
Charlotte, North Carolina
Time Warner Cable, Inc.
Jones Lang LaSalle

FLORIDA CENTER FOR THE ARTS
AND EDUCATION
Orlando, Florida
University of Central Florida
CNL Properties, Inc.
HKS, Inc. / Farmer Baker Barrios Architects

DUKE INTEGRATIVE MEDICINE
DUKE UNIVERSITY MEDICAL CENTER
Durham, North Carolina
Duke University Medical Center

PIER 1 IMPORTS HEADQUARTERS
Fort Worth, Texas
Pier 1 Imports
MBC / Dunn Consultants

NORTH CAROLINA STATE UNIVERSITY
CENTENNIAL CAMPUS N-4 MASTER PLAN
Raleigh, North Carolina
Craig Davis Properties, Inc.

McKINNEY
Durham, North Carolina
McKinney

3700 GLENWOOD
Raleigh, North Carolina
Grubb Ventures LLC

MIDTOWN ATLANTA OFFICE TOWER
Atlanta, Georgia
Holder Properties

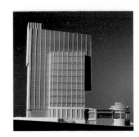

NORTH HILLS OFFICE BUILDING
Raleigh, North Carolina
Kane Realty Corporation

TERMINUS 100
Atlanta, Georgia
Cousins Properties Incorporated

BLUECROSS BLUESHIELD OF TENNESSEE CAMPUS
Chattanooga, Tennessee
BlueCross BlueShield of Tennessee
Jones Lang LaSalle

THE OFFICE BUILDING FOR SURGERY DUKE UNIVERSITY MEDICAL CENTER
Durham, North Carolina
Duke University Medical Center

ELECTRONIC ARTS HEADQUARTERS
Orlando, Florida
Competition Finalist

PUNTO CENTRAL MASTER PLAN
Monterrey, Mexico
Hines

10 TERMINUS PLACE
Atlanta, Georgia
Cousins Properties Incorporated

NORTH HILLS MASTER PLAN
Raleigh, North Carolina
Kane Realty Corporation

PARK CITY MUSASHIKOSUGI
Kanagawa, Japan
Jun Mitsui Architects

SAN ANTONIO RIVERWALK DEVELOPMENT
San Antonio, Texas
Cousins Properties Texas

GLENWOOD MASTER PLAN
Raleigh, North Carolina
Grubb Ventures LLC

TERMINUS MASTER PLAN
Atlanta, Georgia
Cousins Properties Incorporated

350 MISSION STREET
San Francisco, California
Competition Finalist

GALLERIA ARTS DISTRICT MASTER PLAN
Atlanta, Georgia
Cousins Properties Incorporated

TERMINUS 200
Atlanta, Georgia
Cousins Properties Incorporated

**PALISADES WEST
DIMENSIONAL FUND ADVISORS
HEADQUARTERS**
Austin, Texas
Cousins Properties Incorporated

MAIN + GERVAIS OFFICE TOWER
Columbia, South Carolina
Holder Properties

**900 EAST BROUGHTON STREET
SAVANNAH RIVER LANDING**
Savannah, Georgia
Ambling Land & Resort

**DEMOCRACY TOWER
RESTON TOWN CENTER**
Reston, Virginia
Boston Properties, Inc.

PARK CITIES PLAZA
Dallas, Texas
RM Crowe

DALLAS OFFICE TOWER
Dallas, Texas
Hillwood

**1000 EAST BROUGHTON STREET
SAVANNAH RIVER LANDING**
Savannah, Georgia
Ambling Land & Resort

MIAMI OFFICE BUILDING COMPETITION
Miami, Florida
Competition Finalist

**SCHOOL OF PERFORMING ARTS
UNIVERSITY OF CENTRAL FLORIDA**
Orlando, Florida
University of Central Florida

**JAMES B. HUNT JR LIBRARY
NORTH CAROLINA STATE UNIVERSITY**
Raleigh, North Carolina
Competition Finalist

OKLAHOMA CITY COMPETITION
Oklahoma City, Oklahoma
Competition Finalist

AIA NORTH CAROLINA HEADQUARTERS
Raleigh, North Carolina
Competition Finalist

ATLANTA OFFICE TOWER
Atlanta, Georgia

631 NORTH TRYON OFFICE TOWER
Charlotte, North Carolina
First Colony Capital, LLC

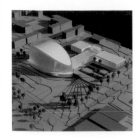

VIRGINIA POLYTECHNIC INSTITUTE & STATE
UNIVERSITY PERFORMING ARTS CENTER
Blacksburg, Virginia
Competition Finalist

UNIVERSITY OF SOUTH FLORIDA
POLYTECHNIC PHASE I
Lakeland, Florida
Competition Finalist

MONTERREY OFFICE BUILDING
Monterrey, Mexico
Hines

110 EMERGENCY SERVICES BUILDING
Dalian, China
City of Dalian

DISCOVERY CENTER, NORTH CAROLINA
SCHOOL OF SCIENCE AND MATHEMATICS
Durham, North Carolina
NC School of Science and Mathematics

DALIAN CITIZEN FITNESS CENTER
Dalian, China
Competition Finalist

NEWMAN CATHOLIC CENTER
DUKE UNIVERSITY
Durham, North Carolina
Duke University

TRENT SEMANS CENTER FOR HEALTH
EDUCATION
DUKE UNIVERSITY SCHOOL OF MEDICINE
Durham, North Carolina
Duke University Medical Center

DREAM OF GREEN
Dalian, China
City of Dalian
Competition Finalist

MIKE CURB COLLEGE OF ARTS, MUSIC AND
SCIENCES BUILDING
DAYTONA STATE COLLEGE
Daytona, Florida
Daytona State College

MCC OFFICE PARK
Dalian, China
MCC

JINZHOU NEW CITY MASTER PLAN
Jinzhou, China
Competition Finalist

TALLEY STUDENT CENTER
NORTH CAROLINA STATE UNIVERSITY
Raleigh, North Carolina
North Carolina State University

RENMIN ROAD OFFICE TOWER
Dalian, China

XI'AN AEROSPACE MUSEUM
Xi'an, China
City of Xi'an

CTECH OFFICE BUILDINGS
Atlanta, Georgia
Cox Enterprises, Inc.
Cousins Properties Incorporated

GRAND ZHONGUA HOTEL
Dalian, China

CHENXI LONGWANGTANG HOTEL
Dalian, China

SHENZHEN NANSHAN TECH CAMPUS
Shenzhen, China

PANYU LANDMARK TOWER
Guangzhou, Guangdong

XI'AN PARK HOTEL
Xi'an, China

EQUUS 333
Monterrey, Mexico
Legado Corporativo S.A. de C.V.

QUIET ROOM, DUKE CANCER CENTER
DUKE UNIVERSITY MEDICAL CENTER
Durham, North Carolina
Duke University Medical Center

ONE FRANKLIN PARK
Franklin, Tennessee
Spectrum Properties / Emery, Inc.

601 MASSACHUSETTS AVENUE
Washington, District of Columbia
Boston Properties, Inc.

COLORADO TOWER
Austin, Texas
Cousins Properties Incorporated

SANCTUARY PARK
Atlanta, Georgia
Jones Lang LaSalle
JP Morgan

CAPITOL RIDGE MASTER PLAN
Austin, Texas

DUKE FACULTY CLUB
Durham, North Carolina
Duke University Faculty Club

DALLAS OFFICE BUILDING
Dallas, Texas
Competition Finalist

BULLIS SCHOOL MASTER PLAN
Potomac, Maryland
Bullis School

WEST END SUMMIT
Nashville, Tennessee
Alex S. Palmer & Company

COX CORPORATE HEADQUARTERS TOWER II
Atlanta, Georgia
Cox Enterprises, Inc.
Cousins Properties Incorporated

PLAZA CONTRY
Monterrey, Mexico
Riverduer

AMERICAN TOBACCO MASTER PLAN, 2012
Durham, North Carolina
Capitol Broadcasting Company

UNIVERSITY OF MANITOBA SUSTAINABLE CAMPUS COMMUNITY
Winnipeg, Canada
Competition

ERWIN TERRACE III
Durham, North Carolina
NEMA Management, LLC

NORTH HILLS TOWER II
Raleigh, North Carolina
Kane Realty Corporation

BULLIS SCHOOL DISCOVERY CENTER
Potomac, Maryland
Bullis School

PHOTOGRAPHY AND BOOK DESIGN CREDITS

PHOTOGRAPHY

JOE AKER, AKER IMAGING HOUSTON
Café Street at Terminus
Palisades West
Pier 1 Imports Headquarters
Terminus

PAUL BARDAGJY:
McKinney

ROBERT BENSON PHOTOGRAPHY
BlueCross BlueShield of Tennessee
Cox Corporate Campus
CTECH Office Park
Duke Integrative Medicine
Gateway Village
Quiet Room, Duke Cancer Center
School of Performing Arts, University of Central Florida
Terminus
Time Warner Cable Headquarters
Trent Semans Center for Health Education, Duke University School of Medicine
Welcome Center, University of North Carolina School of the Arts

BLUE LIME STUDIO, INC.
601 Massachusetts Avenue
Colorado Tower

COLES HAIRSTON
Frost Bank Tower

COUSINS PROPERTIES INCORPORATED
Café Street at Terminus

PATRICK DAVISON
Duda/Paine Architects Studio

TIMOTHY HURSLEY
Cox Corporate Campus
Time Warner Cable Headquarters
Welcome Center, University of North Carolina School of the Arts

TOP*SIDE*FRONT VISUAL ARTISTS
Colorado Tower
Equus 333
Talley Student Center, North Carolina State University

JAMES WEST / JWEST PRODUCTIONS
Gateway Village Technology Center

PATRICK Y. WONG / ATELIER WONG PHOTOGRAPHY
Frost Bank Tower

BOOK DESIGN
Pablo Mandel / CircularStudio.com
Treasure Lathan

This book is the summation of over fifteen years of architectural work and would have been impossible to complete without all the clients, architects, designers and engineers who have participated in bringing form to these projects and to the expression of our ideas. Our thanks go out to them and to our dedicated staff, both past and present.

In particular, we would like to thank our Associates at Duda/Paine, including Russell Holcomb, Dave Davis, Sanjeev Patel, Scott Shell, Brendan Beachler, Lynn Dunn, Darren Lathan, Treasure Lathan, Philip Lozier and Andres Serpa. We would also like to thank those who have contributed specifically to this book, including Treasure Lathan, Scott Baltimore, Gillian Williams, Lynn Dunn and Travis Hicks. Special thanks to our editor, Rebecca Edmunds, whose talents and efforts turned a collection of images and words into a realized book.

— Turan Duda and Jeff Paine

DUDA/PAINE ARCHITECTS

333 Liggett Street
Durham, NC 27701
919.688.5133 t